Love
and
Humility

MARK ALLEN BERRYHILL

WESTBOW
PRESS®
A DIVISION OF THOMAS NELSON
& ZONDERVAN

WestBow Press books may be ordered through booksellers or by contacting:

WestBow Press
A Division of Thomas Nelson & Zondervan
1663 Liberty Drive
Bloomington, IN 47403
www.westbowpress.com
1 (866) 928-1240

Scripture taken from the King James Version of the Bible.

ISBN: 978-1-9736-5222-9 (sc)
ISBN: 978-1-9736-5224-3 (hc)
ISBN: 978-1-9736-5223-6 (e)

Library of Congress Control Number: 2019900871

Print information available on the last page.

WestBow Press rev. date: 1/28/2019

Introduction

Teach the Lord's Word
By Mark Berryhill

We are going to learn the Word of God in this country, and we are going to teach the Lord Jesus Christ's lambs His Word. It is established by the Lord God Almighty, the creator and owner of heaven and earth. Please take the time to read the following:

1. All praise, glory, and honor to God the Father, the Lord Jesus Christ, and the Holy Ghost. _Proverbs 16:1-33_; _Proverbs 3:1-35_; _Proverbs 4:1-27_
2. God exalts nations that diligently seek His righteousness and teach their children the Word of God. _Proverbs 14:34_
3. When a young child walks into his or her school, the first thing he or she should see is the Pledge of Allegiance proudly displayed at the entrance of the school.
4. When children walk into their rooms the first thing they should see proudly displayed on the wall are the Lord God Almighty's Ten Commandments and the Whole Armor of God. _Exodus 20:1-26_; _Ephesians 6:10-24_
5. The first thing that should take place after the first bell. The Lords Prayer. _Matthew 6:9-13_
6. After the Lords Prayer, the Pledge of Allegiance.
7. Our bodies are the Temple of God. _I Corinthians 3:16-17_;_I Corinthians 6:19-20_;_II Corinthians 6:16-18_
8. Things seen were made by an invisible, eternal God. _II Corinthians 4:18_; _II Corinthians 5:1_; _I Timothy 1:17_
9. The following should be placed into effect in all elementary schools, middle schools, and high schools throughout the United States of America immediately. Please study the Word of God daily, also, please study these Scriptures and tell your Christian friends, and have them notify the leaders of the nation immediately.
10. The following:
    1. Two hours of Bible class study for the students in all elementary schools, middle schools, and high schools.
    2. The importance of repentance and baptism in the name of Jesus Christ for the remission of sins, and to receive the gift of the Holy Ghost, and the importance of obedience after baptism.
    3. The importance of regular partaking of the Lord's Supper.

Dear friends,

Place the Pledge of Allegiance at the front of all schools immediately.

Have the Ten Commandments, and the Whole Armor of God placed in each room of the schools today.

Begin the morning by having the children reciting the Lords Prayer, and the Pledge of Allegiance.

The first hour of the day is to be spent in God's Word. A man, not a woman is to teach a one-hour lesson from the Word each morning of the day before the entire faculty and student body.

The grace of our Lord Jesus Christ be with you. Amen.

Thank you,
Mark Berryhill

Teach the Lord's Word

Dear friends,

Have the bands of each school play fifteen minutes of praise and worship music before the lesson and another fifteen minutes after the lesson.

Involve the entire student body and faculty in the praise and worship time each morning.

The grace of our Lord Jesus Christ be with you. Amen.

Thank you,
Mark Berryhill

Dear friends,

In addition to the praise and worship service in the morning the following is also to be placed into effect:

- One hour per day is to be invested in the memorization of Scriptures as follows; 30 minutes in full New Testament chapters, 15 minutes on the most important verse of each New Testament chapter, and 15 minutes on the most important verse of each Old Testament chapter.
- Have another hour of study per day: directly from and out of the Word. This will make a total three hours each day that are to be invested in God's Word for the future of our children.

Note: Women can teach these classes but they are not to teach the early praise and worship service which takes place every morning. This position is ordained by God, for a man to teach.

The following is the list of books, which are to be taught to the different age groups:

Elementary Schools
Old Testament: *Genesis-Chronicles*
New Testament: *Matthew-Galatians*

Middle Schools
Old Testament: *2 Chronicles-Ezekiel*
New Testament: *Ephesians-Philemon*

High Schools
Old Testament *Daniel-Malachi*
New Testament *Hebrews-Revelation*
Note: Place three wooden crosses in the front of each school with a navy flag with white letters, which states: Father, Son and Holy Ghost.

Thank you,
Mark Berryhill

We live in one of the most blessed countries of the world since God created the universe. However, since 1962, the spiritual, moral, and financial decline of our country becomes more evident with each passing day. We become what we practice on a daily basis. When we practice godliness, holiness, and righteousness, we become a godly, holy, and righteous people. Let no man deceive you, if you practice righteousness, you are righteous.

On the other hand, if we and or our children practice ungodliness, unholiness, and unrighteousness, we become an ungodly, unholy, and unrighteous people. Two students recently wrote a school paper concerning the rapid moral decline that is taking place within our country. According to their study, the AIDS virus, and other sexually transmitted diseases have continued to increase at alarming rates in the United States of America over the last several years. The children must be taught God's Word on a daily basis in the public schools. They must be made aware of the struggle between Spirit and flesh, _Galatians 5:16,17_. The children also need to know what the fruit of the Spirit is, _Galatians 5:22,23_. They must be instructed that unless they are married, they are not to be joined together as one, _Galatians 6:7,8,9,10_.

I recently met a young boy named Joshua who is approximately 12 or 13 years of age. I asked him if he could tell me about Joshua in the Bible. His answer was simply stated: who is he? Please read _Joshua 1:8_, _Psalms 1:1,2_ and _Revelation 1:3_. _Romans 10:17_ says, "So then faith cometh by hearing and hearing by the Word of God."[1] In both _Matthew 21:43_ and _Psalms 9:17_, the Lord shares with us what happens to people and nations who walk contrary to His statutes and commandments. Our children are in the public schools being taught anything and everything except what is important, God's Word.

It is extremely important to know the state of the flock at all times, _Proverbs 27:23_. We are responsible and accountable for the daily spiritual growth and moral leadership of the children in this country. What is taking place on many of the college campuses throughout this country? The exact same things that were taking place when God Almighty had Noah build an ark. We must teach our children not only the importance of repentance and baptism in the name of Jesus Christ for the remission of sins, but also the importance of obedience after baptism, _Matthew 28:18,19,20_. The regular partaking of the Lord's Supper is also a must, _John 6:53, 54_. The amount of debt the federal government has acquired since daily prayer and daily Bible class study were withdrawn from the public school systems is an insurmountable amount for man. However, with God in our daily lives, and in the daily lives of our children, it is nothing, for with God all things are possible.

Thank you,
Mark Berryhill

[1]Romans 10:17.

Love and Humility

By Mark Berryhill

Love and Humility

A prayer of Mark Berryhill

Father, what would You have me write about today?

Father, I see a precious three year old boy bowed down on his knees with clasped hands praying fervently unto You.

Father, the words that Your Holy Spirit prayed through the little boy touched my heart and I am overwhelmed by the knowledge You have already filled him with.

Father, the sincerity with which His words are spoken and the love which he already possesses for You causes tears of joy to run down the cheeks of my face.

Father, may You be as close to him today and for all of the tomorrows as the day I saw him kneeled down praying to You with a pure love in His heart for You that I am jealous of.

Father, may the joy that the prayers of our children cause in Your heart last throughout infinite.

Father, may the love that our children possess for You be renewed in our own hearts, and may we learn to walk in the humility that they own.

Father, I see the elderly man at the nursing home sitting in his wheel chair and sadness enters my heart, and yet the sight of the young man caring for him lightens my heart with a smile.

Father, help us to care and provide for the elderly men and women as if they were our newborn babies.

Father, help us to care for the fatherless.

Father, help us to keep ourselves unspotted from the world.

Father, we desire to love You with all of our hearts, souls, minds and strength.

Father, mold us with Your skillful hands and cause us to cleave unto You as none have ever cleaved unto their beloved Father.

In the name of the
Father, the Son and
the Holy Ghost

Amen and Amen
Copyright © 2008

1

A Prayer for the Perfect Wife

A song of Mark Berryhill

Father God, I pray that You will give me a wife that loves You with all of her heart, soul, mind and strength.

Father God, I pray that she loves Your Word with all of her heart, soul, mind and strength.

Father God, I pray that she will love me with all of her heart, soul, mind and strength with a love which is only surpassed by what she has for You.

Father God, I pray that You will give her and me a tribe of little boys that will become ministers of the Gospel of Your Son.

Father God, I pray that You will give her and me a little girl that will be a prophetess in the order of Deborah, Miriam, Hannah, Anna, Elizabeth and even Mary, the mother of Your precious Son Jesus.

Father God, I pray that You will walk with each one of the children as You walked with Jesus while He was here on earth.

Father God, this morning as I prayed to You, tears gently ran down my cheeks.

Father God, this morning I prayed that You would give me a wife that loves me so much that she would lay down her life for me.

Father God, give me a wife that I love so much that I would lay down my life for her.

Father God, You quickly responded to me this morning by saying, now My precious child you understand why I hung on the cross for you.

Father God, You replied, you see My child there is no greater joy and love in the world than for a bridegroom to lay down his life for the wife that He loves with all of His heart, soul, mind and strength.

Father God, give me a wife that will be the perfect wife for me, the perfect mother for our children and the perfect daughter to You.

Father God, place us where we can be most useful for You and Your Word.

In the name of the
Father, the Son and
the Holy Ghost

Amen and Amen
Copyright © 2008

The Walk with Christ

A prayer of Mark Berryhill

The walk with Christ is a joy surpassed by no other!

The walk with Christ will become the reason for waking and the very reason for existing!

The walk with Christ will become as the joy brought into our hearts because of the soft falling rain on a care free afternoon.

The walk with Christ will become as beautiful as the varied colors in God's rainbow which appeared during the rain of the same care-free afternoon.

The walk with Christ is as the brilliance and brightness of one of God's shooting stars as he races across the night sky.

The walk with Christ is as the joy the baby boy brings into my heart each time I hear his precious voice say, "daddy."

The walk with Christ is as the joy the little girl brings into my heart each time I hear her precious voice say, "daddy."

The walk with Christ is as the warmth and joy brought into our hearts each time we enter into our moderate and yet immaculate home that He has provided for us.

The walk with Christ is as the joy brought into our hearts by the Thanksgiving dinner which has been so perfectly prepared.

The walk with Christ is as the view which the eyes present to the mind as we see a magnificent snow-capped mountain of the far north.

The walk with Christ is as the excitement the father experiences as yet another precious child is delicately brought forth from the womb of the mother.

The walk with Christ is as a soothing care-free stroll on a warm summer afternoon at the family farm.

The walk with Christ brings forth joy into our hearts as when a young man realizes that the beautiful young maiden he is head over hills in love with will soon become his wife.

In the name of the
Father, the Son and
the Holy Ghost

Amen and Amen

The Holy Spirit is Love

A song of Mark Berryhill

Holy Spirit, ring forth Your wisdom from Mount Zion throughout the whole earth! Holy Spirit let the children shout forth praises of joy unto You from the rooftops! Holy Spirit, exalted Spirit of the true and living God, set the world on fire for the King of kings!

Holy Spirit, as God's gently falling rain brings forth an abundance of food for His people, so let Your wisdom be shed forth into the hearts of our precious children!

Holy Spirit, as the beauty of God's brilliantly displayed rainbow causes our children's eyes to sparkle with excitement, so let Your pure love be living and active in pure hearts and lives!

Holy Spirit, You are becoming our love, life, hope and joy!

Holy Spirit, touch our hearts with the true and pure love of the Everlasting Father!

Holy Spirit, so as the beauty of the American Bald Eagle as he soars through the firmament of heaven, so let the joy of our living daily for You become the goal of each of Your children!

Holy Spirit, let Your peace be echoed throughout the world of mankind, and may He become the standard by which we choose to live!

Holy Spirit, let Your patience be echoed and felt throughout the world of mankind, and may He dwell within our hearts!

Holy Spirit let the gentleness displayed by Your heart and tongue become the goal for each one of us!

Holy Spirit let Your goodness dwell within our hearts, and let Him be felt throughout the world in its entirety!

Holy Spirit, shed forth Your faith into the hearts of our children, and bless them with faith as the Blessed Trinity's faith!

Holy Spirit, cause Your meekness to live in our hearts, and let Him dwell therein forevermore!

Holy Spirit let our self-control control the hearts and minds of Your called-out children, and let Him have His way in our daily lives!

In the name of the
Father, the Son and
the Holy Ghost

Amen and Amen
Copyright © 2008

4

The Children Belong to JESUS

A song of Mark Berryhill

Children are the greatest creation the Everlasting Father has ever created.
Children are the reason for His existence.
Children are the great reward and delight of the Father's heart of gold.
Children and their smiles make God's life worth living.
Children and their prayers touch the heart of their Creator and His voice roars as the voice of many waters, be fruitful and multiply.
Children and their love for their puppies, kittens and bunny rabbits create joy in the heart of their Creator.
Children, and their love and humility produce a smile on the heart of their Creator that reaches from the farthest star of the east unto the farthest star of the west.
Children are the perfect gift from the perfect giver of gifts, the LORD JEHOVAH God.
Children and their goodness make our steps lighter and cause the angels to sing songs of beauty concerning them.
Children and their sweetness make for a sweeter life.
Children and their smiles brighten even the darkest of days.
Children, when they are newborn, are so beautiful and helpless and yet in a moment of time they become the new generation of Christ's leaders.
Children, when they have become unable to care for themselves because of time and the elements thereof, are still to be treated with the love and compassion demonstrated toward the newborn child.
Children are children in the eyes of the Everlasting Father whether we are newborn or 120 years old.

In the name of the
Father, the Son and
the Holy Ghost

Amen and Amen
Copyright © 2008

Jesus Christ the Same Yesterday, and Today, and Forever

A song of Mark Berryhill

Jesus Christ has become the joy of our life!

Jesus Christ has become the reason for every moment of every season!

Jesus Christ is the same yesterday, and today, and forever!

Jesus Christ is our love, life, hope and joy!

Jesus Christ saved me when I was twelve years old!

Jesus Christ walked me to the baptistery by the power of the Holy Ghost and caused me to accept Him as my personal Savior!

Jesus Christ, my precious friend is not in the abandoning of souls business!

Jesus Christ loves you with all of His heart, soul, mind and strength!

Jesus Christ, direct our steps in the pathway of holiness and righteousness for Your great names sake!

Jesus Christ, let the voices of the children be heard from the rooftops glorifying Your holy name!

Jesus Christ, thank You for the sun, the moon and the innumerable brilliant racing stars!

Jesus Christ, teach us how to love You with all of our hearts, souls, minds and strength!

Jesus Christ, thank You for the precious gift of the newborn child!

Jesus Christ, thank You for the health that we enjoy today!

Jesus Christ, thank You for the gift of laughter and the beauty of a precious child's smile!

Jesus Christ, thank You for the cool and refreshing breeze!

Jesus Christ, thank you for the gift and power of the Holy Ghost!

Jesus Christ, thank You for another day to serve You with a pure and contrite heart!

Jesus Christ, anoint these precious lambs with the spirit of love, joy, peace, longsuffering, gentleness, goodness, faith, meekness and temperance!

In the name of the
Father, the Son and
the Holy Ghost

Amen and Amen
Copyright © 2008

True Understanding

A prayer of Mark Berryhill

When He was in pain did you extend your hand unto Him or look the other way?

When the young maiden found herself with child and a boyfriend who denied the affair, did you extend the help she needed or look the other way?

When the young man was broke and down on his luck because of no fault of his own did you offer the money he needed or look the other way?

When our decisions are based on monetary concerns rather than spiritual needs, we need to look the other way.

When the next drink of alcohol becomes more of a desire than spending time with the precious bride of your youth, repent, and direct your thoughts toward Christ.

When watching television is more important to you than studying God's Word, reconsider your priorities.

When our every thought is brought into the captivity of Jesus Christ and His Word we then will possess understanding!

In the name of the
Father, the Son and
the Holy Ghost

Amen and Amen
Copyright © 2008

Love, Love, Love

A prayer of Mark Berryhill

The true love which Christ possesses for you will endure throughout infinite.
The true love which Christ possesses for His called-out children is as the beauty of a slender fawn prancing eloquently through the nearby open field.
The true love which Christ possesses for His faithful children is as the joy a father experiences the first time his precious daughter calls him "daddy."
The true love which Christ possesses for you is as the sound of laughter heard in a room when a father has told a wonderful and yet humorous story.
The true love which Christ possesses for His precious child is as the joy a husband experiences while hugging his wife after a long absence from her.
The true love which Christ possesses for His precious child is as the beauty of the picturesque scene of the great white capped mountains of the far north.
The true love which Christ possesses for the child is as the joy a mother experiences when her son calls her "mommy" for the first time.
The true love which Christ possesses for His child is as the power and fury of a great hurricane as he makes his way from the waters of the deep towards the isolated island.
The true love which Christ possesses for His lambs was most accurately demonstrated while He hung on the cross with outstretched arms thereby signifying, "I love you with all that I AM."

In the name of the
Father, the Son and
the Holy Ghost

Amen and Amen
Copyright © 2008

The Joy of Life

A prayer of Mark Berryhill

The man reminded me of a great grizzly bear of the far north when I first saw him.

His arms were huge and at first glance I thought to myself, most people would fear this man because of his great size.

A few moments later I looked over at the same man and he was holding one of the most precious babies that I have ever seen.

The man with the apparent great strength was suddenly turned into a piece of clay once his granddaughter was handed over to him.

The previous frowns and hard looks of the man were suddenly translated into delicate kisses and hugs for a precious granddaughter.

The Great God that formed you in the womb of your mother loves you with all of His heart, soul, mind and strength.

The Great God that formed you in the womb of your mother is not in the forsaking of souls business.

The Great God that created life, light and hope is your best friend and His hand reaches down from Heaven and is always open and ready to receive His loved ones.

The Great God that fearfully and wonderfully created you pays attention to the details of His children even from before conception until after the victory of death of those who diligently seek Him, love Him and obey Him.

The Great God that has been loving and rescuing His called-out children for approximately 6,500 years has become the love of our lives.

The Great God that created the precious baby girl that you will tuck in bed tonight truly is a Father who possesses a heart of pure gold.

Holy Father, walk us in the light of Your Son Jesus Christ.

In the name of the
Father the Son and
the Holy Ghost

Amen and Amen
Copyright © 2008

Walking in the Light of Christ

A song of Mark Berryhill

Jesus Christ is love. Jesus Christ is life. Jesus Christ is hope. Jesus Christ is our strength. Jesus Christ is our strong tower. Jesus Christ is our refuge.

Jesus Christ and His Spirit is the sparkle of light in the baby girl when she says I love you "daddy" for the first time.

Jesus Christ and His Spirit causes faithful fathers to carry disobedient children when it would have seemed easier to have looked the other way.

Jesus Christ is the way, the truth, the life and besides Him there is no other.

Jesus Christ is only a prayer away. If you need Him, give Him a call or if you just want to tell Him that you love Him and thank Him for everything that will be great also.

Jesus Christ, fill our hearts with Your faith, Your confidence and cause us to boldly proclaim Your Word throughout the whole earth.

Jesus Christ, we love You and we need You!

Jesus Christ, thank You for saving us!

Jesus Christ, thank You for healing us!

Jesus Christ, thank You for Your great discipline at the cross!

Jesus Christ, fill our children's hearts with You!

In the name of the
Father, the Son and
the Holy Ghost

Amen and Amen
Copyright © 2008

Jesus Christ is Love

A song of Mark Berryhill

Jesus Christ is faithful and He is true!

Jesus Christ is the light of the world!

Jesus Christ is our strength, strong tower and refuge!

Jesus Christ is the comfort for those who need to be comforted!

Jesus Christ and His Spirit is now the helping hand for the seemingly hopeless and helpless drunkards!

Jesus Christ owns the next breath of life that you breathe!

Jesus Christ is the hope for the seemingly hopeless!

Jesus Christ is the life for all men!

Jesus Christ and serving Him will become the very reason for our existence!

Jesus Christ is love!

Jesus Christ touches hearts and changes lives the way no other can!

Jesus Christ, we love You!

Jesus Christ, we need You!

Jesus Christ, we adore You!

Jesus Christ, glorify Your great and matchless name throughout all the earth!

Jesus Christ and His Word will become our life!

Jesus Christ, thank You for turning the sadness in our hearts to joy!

Jesus Christ, thank You for the gift and avenue of prayer!

Jesus Christ, thank You for the precious gift of our children!

Jesus Christ, as You are placed in the bosom of our Father, so place these precious little lambs in Your bosom!

Jesus Christ is the way, the truth and the life, and beside Him there is no other!

In the name of the
Father, the Son and
the Holy Ghost

Amen and Amen
Copyright © 2008

A Reason to Smile

A prayer of Mark Berryhill

Holy Ghost, be glorified throughout all of the earth!

Holy Ghost, set the world on fire for Jesus Christ, the King of kings!

Holy Ghost, thank You for the gift and avenue of prayer!

Holy Ghost, thank You for the air that we breathe!

Holy Ghost, thank You for the creation!

Holy Ghost, thank You for the precious gift of our children!

Holy Ghost, transform our minds into the mind of Jesus Christ!

Holy Ghost, cause the magnificence of Your face to shine brilliantly throughout all of the earth, days, months and years without end!

Holy Ghost, bless the works of our hands and the works of our children's hands!

Holy Ghost, may you be exalted from sea to sparkling sea and from the lowest of the valleys unto the tallest of mountains!

Holy Ghost, write Your love on our hearts with Your finger and mold us with Your skillful hands!

Holy Ghost, place discipline back into the daily lives of our children!

Holy Ghost, lead us, love us and prove our hearts!

Holy Ghost, teach us your ways and walk us in the light of Jesus Christ!

Holy Ghost, cause Your beautiful smile to be ever-present before our spiritual eyes!

Holy Ghost, bless these precious lambs of Jesus Christ!

Holy Ghost, bless these precious lambs of Jesus Christ!

Holy Ghost, bless these precious lambs of Jesus Christ!

Holy Ghost, bless these precious lambs of Jesus Christ!

Holy Ghost, You are our love, light and very reason for existence!

Holy Ghost, You are blessed because of all of these precious lambs!

Holy Ghost, we love You, we need You and now we adore You!

In the name of the
Father, the Son and
the Holy Ghost

Amen and Amen
Copyright © 2008

Love is From God

A song of Mark Berryhill

Holy Ghost, in our lives there are struggles and obstacles, and yet the victories and success that you cause are priceless.

Holy Ghost, there is a world of children that need to know who You are!

Holy Ghost, help us to get to the children, and to get them taught Your pure Word every day!

Holy Ghost, cause these words to flow into our hearts as Your peaceful rivers flow from the high ground to the lowest of valleys.

Holy Ghost, may You be exalted as the Father, and the Son are exalted!

Holy Ghost, may You become loved as the Father and the Son are loved!

Holy Ghost, fill us with the Word of knowledge and the Word of wisdom.

Holy Ghost, mold these precious lambs of Christ Jesus with the skill You provide the brilliant surgeon as he so precisely repairs damage caused to a loved one.

Holy Ghost, cause Your love to flow from Heaven, even more wonderfully than as Your rain pours down from the dark gray overshadowing cloud.

Holy Ghost, as the precious blood ran down the cheeks of God's lamb while He was hanging on the cross, so let Your infinite love flow into our hearts.

Holy Ghost, so as the smile of a precious two year old baby girl touches our hearts with joy, so let our joy of seeking You be our reason for waking each morning.

Holy Ghost, so as the wind gently whispers as he glides through the gorgeous pine trees of the tallest of white capped mountains, so let Your voice be the lead of Your called-out children.

Holy Ghost, so as the great bear has captured his prey as his huge claws snatched the fish out of the running river, so let Your heart's goal be to win the heart's of Your children.

Holy Ghost, write love and joy into our hearts with Your finger, and erase hate and sadness from within our hearts.

Holy Ghost, let the brilliance and majesty of Your love be felt and seen from one side of the universe unto the other side.

Holy Ghost, as the anointed artist brings to life the beauty of the gorgeous untouched wilderness in his painting, so let the beauty of Your smile be ever present before our spiritual eyes.

In the name of the
Father, the Son and
the Holy Ghost

Amen and Amen
Copyright © 2008

13

True Faith

A song of Mark Berryhill

True faith in Christ produces hope for the seemingly hopeless.

True faith in Christ transforms hate into love.

True faith in Christ will cause Him to open windows of Heaven for you, and cause you not to have room for all of the blessings He bestows upon you!

True faith in Christ causes frowns to turn into smiles.

True faith in Christ makes one realize that the day of one's death is better than the day of one's birth.

True faith in Christ is a gift from the Father of lights, and comes through the diligent study of the greatest book that has ever been written, The Word of God.

True faith in Christ opens ones spiritual eyes and closes ones eyes toward the world.

True faith in Christ makes one realize the need to replenish the earth with children, and the importance of raising them as ministers and minister's wives.

True faith in Christ will cause joy in your heart when it would seem that there is no joy to be found.

True faith in Christ causes one to leap for joy and shout, Father; I love You with all that I am!

True faith in Christ makes one come to the final realization that Christ has everything under control, JEHOVAH is sovereign!

True faith in Christ transforms ones tears of sadness into tears of joy!

True faith in Christ makes us want to sing and dance and tell You that we love You, Immanuel!

In the name of the
Father, the Son and
the Holy Ghost

Amen and Amen
Copyright © 2008

Within the Heart of Man

A song of Mark Berryhill

Within the heart of man there are treasures untold.

Within the heart of man there is love which has yet to be explored.

Within the heart of man there are pictures of beauty which have yet to be painted.

Within the heart of man there is love which has yet to flow as the running rivers of the Almighty flow.

Within the heart of man there is love which neither gold nor silver can be compared unto.

Within the heart of man there is such great love and faithfulness that when he is called by JEHOVAH to sacrifice his life for a friend he will obey the Father's voice.

Within the heart of man there are pictures of silver and gold which have yet to be discovered.

Within the heart of man there are pictures of mountains that reach into the Heavens and valleys that reach down into the very heart of the earth.

Within the heart of man there is a desire to care for and share with the less fortunate.

Within the heart of man is the hope and determination for a better life because of our Lord and Savior Jesus Christ.

Within the heart of man there is love, joy, peace, longsuffering, gentleness, goodness, faith, meekness and temperance.

Within the heart of man there exists a love and craving for the Creator which can only be described by stating, Father, we love You with all that we are!

Within the heart of man there is good and there is evil, and yet I pray that good will become the desire of the heart of each man.

Within the heart of man there is compassion and mercy because man is created in the likeness and image of a compassionate and merciful Father.

Within the heart of man is the hope for a future of beautiful children who will become tomorrow's kings and priests.

Within the heart of man the picture reveals a life full of joy seeking the Great I AM!

Within the heart of man the picture is revealed of an eternity spent in paradise with the Blessed Trinity.

In the name of the
Father, the Son and
the Holy Ghost

Amen and Amen
Copyright © 2008

Thank You Father

A song of Mark Berryhill

Holy Father, thank You for the beautiful weather that You provide us with during this time of the year!

Holy Father, thank you for the precious baby birds which offer songs of beauty and praise unto both You and our ears!

Holy Father, thank You for the place where we will lay our tired heads this very night!

Holy Father, thank You for providing another day of work!

Holy Father, thank You for the beauty which is presented to our eyes as Your magnificent sun begins his ascent each morning!

Holy Father, thank You for the beauty which is presented to our eyes as Your magnificent sun begins his descent in the far west!

Holy Father, thank you for Immanuel!

Holy Father, thank You for carrying our precious lambs today!

Holy Father, thank You for the gift of our precious children!

Holy Father, thank You for the health that we enjoy today!

Holy Father, thank You for writing the greatest book that has ever been written, Your Word!

Holy Father, thank you for the gift of the Holy Ghost, and the comfort that He brings into our lives!

Holy Father, thank You for love, joy, peace, longsuffering, gentleness, goodness faith, meekness and temperance!

Holy Father, thank You for showing us the correct pathway!

Holy Father, thank You for equipping Your people with the Sword of the Spirit!

Holy Father, thank You for the beauty of Your creation!

Holy Father, thank You for pure hearts, mold our hearts into hearts of gold and into hearts of silver!

Holy Father, thank You for dreams and visions!

Holy Father, thank You for every part that makes up our fearfully and wonderfully made bodies!

Holy Father, thank You for love, life, joy and happiness!

Holy Father, You are brilliant!

In the name of the
Father, the Son and
the Holy Ghost

Amen and Amen
Copyright © 2008

Immanuel is Love

A song of Mark Berryhill

Love is a word too seldom spoken.

Love is a word that changed the world as the world was known.

Love is a word that expresses the beauty felt within the heart of a mother as she lovingly cradles her newborn baby girl!

Love is a word that expresses how a father feels about his precious and adorable four year old son as the son is humbly bowed down with clasped hands praying fervently to his Beloved Father!

Love is a word which brings forth unexplained joy into the hearts of those it is spoken to.

Love is a word which has the power of the flowing rivers of the Almighty which are roaring and racing after one of His mighty downpours.

Love is word which causes the hearts of young married lovers to leap with excitement and joy!

Love is a word that says we need You forevermore Immanuel!

Love is a word that causes us to continually thank the Father of lights for the greatest gift He has ever created, the newborn child.

In the name of the
Father, the Son and
the Holy Ghost

Amen and Amen
Copyright © 2008

A Child in a Manger

A song of Mark Berryhill

JEHOVAH's love for the children can be neither weighed nor measured.

JEHOVAH's love for the children is as the beauty of a precious little girl in a pretty new dress as she presents you with her most beautiful of smiles.

JEHOVAH's love for the children is as the artists painting, which brings to life the beauty of a fresh new day as God's brilliant golden sun rises in the east.

JEHOVAH's love for the children is as the artists painting which illustrates the brilliance of God's pink and golden sun as he sets in the far west.

JEHOVAH's love for the children is as a four thousand member band playing in perfect precision and harmony, glorifying the LORD of the armies of the angels of Heaven.

JEHOVAH's love for the children is as the beauty of a precious eight year old daughter as she recites the twenty-third Psalms from memory for her first time.

JEHOVAH's love for the children is as a scene of two precious little bunnies, one black and one white, hopping across the recently cut lawn.

JEHOVAH's love for the children is as the scene of a brilliant and beautiful musician as she pours her heart out to her God in song.

JEHOVAH's love for the children is as an eternal love which will cause His called-out children to pray for their little ones forever.

JEHOVAH's love for the children is as the beauty of love and humility demonstrated by a beloved four year old son.

JEHOVAH's love for the children is as the beat of a jockey's heart seconds before the opening of the horse races starting gate.

JEHOVAH's love for the children is as the beauty of the scene of a newly born baby girl being lovingly cradled by her first time mother.

JEHOVAH's love for the children is as the spiritual picture of our Father's smile which reaches from the farthest star of the west unto the farthest star of the east.

JEHOVAH's love for the children is as the scene of a dozen ducks excitedly playing on the lake during a crisp cold December morning.

JEHOVAH's love for the children is as the beauty of the song the wind sings as he races through the great pine trees of a beautiful wooded forest.

JEHOVAH's love for the children is as the picture of a new daddy holding his first born son ever so closely to his heart.

JEHOVAH's love for the children is as the scene of a precious newborn baby boy placed safely between his mother and daddy in a manger in the city known as Bethlehem.

In the name of the
Father, the Son and
the Holy Ghost

Amen and Amen
Copyright © 2008

18

JEHOVAH Is Worthy of all of the Praise!

A song of Mark Berryhill

JEHOVAH is faithful and there is none with a pure heart as is with the heart of JEHOVAH!

JEHOVAH is great and there is none who can be compared unto JEHOVAH!

JEHOVAH is love and there is none who displays the beauty of kindness like unto JEHOVAH!

JEHOVAH created this magnificent universe and within His right hand ballerinas perform their most brilliant performances while concentrating on JEHOVAH!

JEHOVAH spoke and created light, and who breathed life into His son Adam as did our JEHOVAH?

JEHOVAH blesses us, loves us, and cradles us within His heart whether we are awake or asleep for this is the very character of our JEHOVAH!

JEHOVAH's gentleness causes butterflies to flutter as they seemingly perform dances of faithfulness to each other within the very palm of our LORD JEHOVAH!

JEHOVAH, with His gentleness, forms the beautiful and yet helpless child within the womb of the mother, and will carry the precious child all of her days because He is JEHOVAH!

JEHOVAH dwells in an unapproachable light, and yet He also dwells in darkness because there is none who can be likened unto our King the LORD JEHOVAH!

JEHOVAH's love for His children can not be expressed with the words that I write because He, our LORD JEHOVAH, created love, and that word is the very word that best describes JEHOVAH!

JEHOVAH, we love You, we need You, we praise You, and we glorify You, be Abba unto us forevermore LORD JEHOVAH!

JEHOVAH, transform the hearts and minds of these precious lambs into the likeness of Jesus Christ, and like unto you, LORD JEHOVAH!

JEHOVAH, let Your love and Your presence be felt from sea unto sea, and from the lowest of valleys unto the tallest of Your mountains LORD JEHOVAH!

JEHOVAH, help us to set the world on fire for Jesus, and cause our days to be spent walking beside You and talking with You, oh LORD JEHOVAH!

JEHOVAH, there is none as faithful as You, and we thank You from the farthest star of the west unto the farthest star of the east for Your great faithfulness unto us LORD JEHOVAH!

In the name of the
Father, the Son and
the Holy Ghost

Amen and Amen
Copyright © 2008

An Ornament of Grace

A song of Mark Berryhill

Jesus Christ is the light of the world!

Jesus Christ is the love within the hearts of His called-out children!

Jesus Christ is the hope for the hopeless!

Jesus Christ fills our hearts with joy because of His Word and our children!

Jesus Christ will never ever leave nor forsake His called-out children.

Jesus Christ created faithfulness, and within that very word His character is most accurately described!

Jesus Christ gave His life for you and for me because of His great love and faithfulness to His children!

Jesus Christ gently whispers, I love you My child, feed My precious lambs!

Jesus Christ stands tall between the cherubim's!

Jesus Christ stands tall between the tallest of the earth's mountains!

Jesus Christ is the Shepherd and Bishop of our souls!

Jesus Christ is the way, the truth, and the life, and besides Him there is no other!

Jesus Christ is eternal life!

Jesus Christ is eternal love!

Jesus Christ is the creator of life, the sustainer of life, and the giver of eternal life!

Jesus Christ, You are awesome and worthy to receive all of the praise!

Jesus Christ, thank You for the love, beauty, and goodness our precious children bring into our lives!

Jesus Christ, the same yesterday, and today, and forever!

Jesus Christ, thank You for an ornament of grace, and the crown of glory you wore for Your lambs!

Jesus Christ transforms tears of hurt and pain into tears of joy and love, walk with Him!

In the name of the
Father, the Son and
the Holy Ghost

Amen and Amen
Copyright © 2008

The Beauty of God's Eternal Spirit

A prayer of Mark Berryhill

The woman sitting on the porch of the old farm house has a face which appears as the face of an elderly Indian woman.

Her nose is large and her face is square in shape; because of her blessed ninety nine years of life from her God, her skin remains to appear soft, and yet has begun to droop significantly.

The picture that I want to share with you about her is the picture that she always presented to me. She had one true desire in life, and her hearts desire was for everyone to know Jesus and His Word.

As one would converse with her, the conversation would inevitably be invested in what she loved most, or rather about who she loved most, Jesus Christ!

Father, thank You for great-grandmothers!

Father, thank You for the fervent prayers of great-grandmothers and their love for You!

Father, thank You for the great example my great-grandmother was to me and to each one of her family members!

Father, her great love for You can still be felt even within my heart!

Father, You are brilliant, and You deserve all of the praise, glory and honor!

Father, glorify Your holy name throughout all of the earth!

Father, thank You for our children!

Father, thank You for great-grandmothers who loved and served You with every fiber of their being!

In the name of the
Father, the Son and
the Holy Ghost

Amen and Amen
Copyright © 2008

The Beauty of Life

A prayer of Mark Berryhill

The farm is beautiful, and consists of many open fields with freshly cut green grass.

There are numerous ponds filled with fish, and creeks which run various routes throughout the picturesque and tranquil terrain.

The magnificent and huge lake is within a rocks throw from the old farm house which is called the old home place.

A huge tree which was struck by one of God's arrows of lightning and fallen creates what appears as a beautifully designed wood bridge.

Small, medium sized and large trees surround what is known as the old home place, and are populous along the gentle flowing creeks.

A picture introduced by God shows a young man walking through a field with a precious little fluffy white lamb cuddling next to the man's leg and apparently craving all of his attention.

At the far side of one of the fields are two huge bulls and a cow. Each of them are brown in color and of great strength and excellent health.

Fences surround the property merely to keep the cattle from straying onto someone else's property or from entering onto the nearby highway.

The beauty of God's brilliant creation is too often taken for granted. May we learn to fully appreciate the brilliance of His genius.

Life is a race which passes so quickly and yet if we run the race investing everything for Christ, we suddenly discover an indescribable joy for living!

We are created for one reason, and that reason is to serve our Lord Jesus Christ with all that we are!

Father, thank You for these fearfully and wonderfully made lambs!

Father, teach us how to love You with every fiber of our being!

Father, may Your face be ever present before our spiritual eyes!

In the name of the
Father, the Son and
the Holy Ghost

Amen and Amen
Copyright © 2008

Abba, Abba

A song of Mark Berryhill

Elohim let Your words of beauty flow from Heaven as Your rivers flow from the high ground to the lowest of valleys!

El Shaddai, as You saved Your son Isaac from the knife which was placed within Your friend Abraham's hand, so save our great nation!

Adonai, so as You rewarded Abraham's great faithfulness and obedience to Your voice in offering Isaac as a sacrifice unto You, reward us for Your Son's discipline at the cross by opening our spiritual eyes, and training our spiritual ears to know Your voice!

Yahweh, bless the works of our hands, and bless the works of our children's hands.

JEHOVAH, You are our life and light, and to serve You is our very reason for existence!

As the American Bald Eagle soars on the wings of the angels of the Everlasting Father, so let our love for You soar with You eternally!

J.A.H., as You ride upon the wind and as You glide from one side of the universe unto the other, so let Your eternal love for Your lambs break through into their hearts and minds, and comfort them forevermore!

He is just a prayer away, and if you are in need call Him, His name is Wonderful Counselor!

The thunder roars and the Lion of Judah utters His voice, I love the children, I love the children, I love the children!

Prince of Peace, thank You for the peace that You bring into our lives!

He is the Beginning and He is the End, He is Alpha and Omega!

Worthy to be praised is the Lamb of God, for He and He alone won the race for mankind!

JESUS CHRIST, thank You for Your Word, for Your Holy Spirit and for our lambs!

Abba, touch our hearts with the eternal fire of Your finger, and set the ship on course for eternal life!

In the name of the
Father, the Son and
the Holy Ghost

Amen and Amen
Copyright © 2008

23

JEHOVAH, JESUS and the HOLY GHOST

A prayer of Mark Berryhill

JEHOVAH, JESUS and the HOLY GHOST are undefeatable!

JEHOVAH, JESUS and the HOLY GHOST are the righteousness of our lives!

JEHOVAH, JESUS and the HOLY GHOST sing songs of beauty and raindrops begin pouring down from Heaven above!

JEHOVAH, JESUS and the HOLY GHOST are the joy of life!

JEHOVAH, JESUS and the HOLY GHOST give us our best friends!

JEHOVAH, JESUS and the HOLY GHOST cause pine trees to grow tall and beautiful!

JEHOVAH, JESUS and the HOLY GHOST created everything beautiful and we must learn to enjoy their creation!

JEHOVAH, JESUS and the HOLY GHOST place love in hearts which were once hard and calloused because of life's cares and burdens!

JEHOVAH, JESUS and the HOLY GHOST will soon cause you to love these precious lambs the way He does!

JEHOVAH, JESUS and the HOLY GHOST possess the heart of gold!

JEHOVAH, JESUS and the HOLY GHOST anoint musicians with such great talent, take notice of them, better yet; maybe you are one of them!

JEHOVAH, JESUS and the HOLY GHOST, are all powerful!

JEHOVAH, JESUS and the HOLY GHOST will train these precious lambs in the Spirit!

JEHOVAH, JESUS and the HOLY GHOST are to be exalted because they are worthy!

JEHOVAH, JESUS and the HOLY GHOST will write His perfect Word in the hearts and minds of our children!

In the name of the
Father, the Son and
the Holy Ghost

Amen and Amen
Copyright © 2008

Victory at the Cross

A prayer of Mark Berryhill

Lord Jesus, what did You see as You hung from the cross known as Calvary?

Lord Jesus, what went through Your mind as You hung from the cross known as Calvary?

Lord Jesus, as tears of agony flowed down Your cheeks as running rivers of water, how great was the joy You experienced at the victory of the cross?

Lord Jesus, as blood gushed from the holes in Your forehead caused by cruel thorns, explain to me how great it was knowing that You had become the CONQUERER?

Lord Jesus, how much joy entered into Your heart as You proved to the world that no greater love has any man than to lay down his life for the ones he loves!

Lord Jesus, as You hung on the cross did You see Your rich blood redeeming the Father's lambs back unto Him?

Lord Jesus, as You hung on the cross did You ever dream that so many precious little lambs would love You so much?

Lord Jesus, as You hung on the cross did You see the precious little girl two thousand years later tell her daddy with great pain in her heart that the mean men had crucified the Lord she loves!

Lord Jesus, thank You for giving Your children hearts of gold and hearts of silver!

Lord Jesus, thank You for the eternal victory You won at Your cross!

Lord Jesus, as You dwell in an unapproachable light, so may Your Spirit dwell in our hearts!

In the name of the
Father, the Son and
the Holy Ghost

Amen and Amen
Copyright © 2008

Jesus and a Helping Hand

A song of Mark Berryhill

Jesus extended the helping hand to the brother in need while every one else pretended not to see the brothers needs.

Jesus went to the cross because His love for you is immeasurable.

Jesus saw eternity conquered while hanging on the cross known as Calvary.

Jesus wants you to love Him with all of your heart, with all of your soul, with all of your mind and with all of your strength.

Jesus wants you to know that He will never leave nor forsake you, He is faithful and He is true.

Jesus, thank You for these precious children that You have entrusted us with.

Jesus, thank You for the memory of seeing great-grandmothers studying their Bibles on the front porch of their little farm houses.

Jesus, thank You for the Christmas season, I pray that You will cause every day to be celebrated and set apart as Your day!

Jesus, I pray that You will love these precious lambs with all of Your soul, with all of Your mind, and with all of Your strength.

Jesus, let Your presence and love for these children be felt and demonstrated from sea unto shining sea!

Jesus, teach us to be the friend who extends the helping hand to the brother in need while the others pretend not to see that he is in need.

In the name of the
Father, the Son and
the Holy Ghost

Amen and Amen
Copyright © 2008

26

In the Footsteps of Christ

A song of Mark Berryhill

When hope is almost lost and there seems to be no where to turn, wait on the LORD.

When expenses are running at a faster pace than income, consider that wisdom is better than gold and understanding is more valued than silver.

When the man who appears to be of great wealth because of his earthly possessions, consider that eternal life with the Father is the only true great possession.

When a person earns a fortune and then loses a fortune, consider that the only goal worth investing your time in is saving souls.

When the world tells you that it is alright to drink, tell the world that John the Baptist did not.

When the world tells you that using tobacco won't hurt you, go visit your precious brother who is in the hospital dying of the cancer that is ravaging his body.

When the world tells you that sex outside of marriage is acceptable, tell them that adulterers will not inherit the kingdom of God.

When the world tells you that you don't need to study God's Word DAILY, let your voice ring forth to the world, Christ and His Word is my DAILY life.

When your best friend has lost hope because death for Him is just a step away, consider that at death the Victor of Eternal life will be there for you with open arms!

When you loan to the poor, consider that you are loaning unto the Lord.

When you wake up and realize that your life has passed you by, and you didn't serve Christ DAILY, consider and tell your children not to follow in your footsteps.

When you are having a perfect journey with your LORD here on earth, consider that as it is in Heaven so shall it be on earth.

In the name of the
Father, the Son and
The Holy Ghost

Amen and Amen
Copyright © 2008

The Beauty of America

A song of Mark Berryhill

Father, cause our lives to be invested in the diligent daily study of Your Word.
Father, cause our hearts to be filled with Your love and with Your knowledge.
Father, cause our hearts to beat with Your heart.
Father, cause our children to know You the way no other generation of children have ever known You.
Father, cause the beauty of Your smile to rest upon this great nation we call America.
Father, cause the hearts of our children to beat with Your heart.
Father, cause Your face to be what we seek from the rising of the sun until the setting of the sun.
Father, cause husbands to love their wives, and wives to love their husbands as You love Your church, which is Your lambs.
Father, bless the works of our hands, and bless the works of our children's hands.
Father, let Your love flow from Heaven as You cause the great down pour of rain.
Father, we bless You, we love You and we glorify You because You are our all in all.
Father, thank You for the gift of the child, thank You for the Messiah.
Father, thank You for talents yet undiscovered.
Father, thank You for friendships that are yet unknown.
Father, thank You for love, life and most of all, thank You for redeeming us back to You by the blood of the lamb.

In the name of the
Father, the Son and
the Holy Ghost

Amen and Amen
Copyright © 2008

28

JEHOVAH is Love II

A prayer of Mark Berryhill

JEHOVAH reigns over the universe because no other can rule over the universe as does JEHOVAH!

JEHOVAH is Father of all because He is worthy to receive all of the praise, glory, riches and honor because He and He alone is worthy to be called JEHOVAH!

JEHOVAH is love and the Creator of love because love transformed means JEHOVAH!

JEHOVAH spreads forth forgiveness because no other loves you enough to offer His own Son as did the LORD GOD JEHOVAH!

JEHOVAH gives hope to the seemingly hopeless because for a moment as His Son hung on the cross hopelessness was felt in the heart of JEHOVAH!

JEHOVAH cares for you as He does for His own Son for no other understands true love as does JEHOVAH!

JEHOVAH sheds forth joy into the hearts of His people because to give joy to His people places joy in the very heart of JEHOVAH!

JEHOVAH turns hate into love, and frowns into smiles because love and happy are two words which most accurately describe the Great LORD JEHOVAH!

JEHOVAH reaches down from Heaven by the power of His right hand and offers salvation unto the world by the blood of a worthy lamb who is the prized possession of the LORD JEHOVAH!

JEHOVAH is the light of the world, and no other has ever spoken and created light as did our LORD JEHOVAH!

JEHOVAH and His Word offer everything that we need in life because in the beginning as with God and the Word was the LORD GOD JEHOVAH!

In the name of the
Father, the Son and
the Holy Ghost

Amen and Amen
Copyright © 2008

Christ's Love is His Power

A song of Mark Berryhill

Jesus Christ sheds forth love into the hearts of his children because His unfathomable love cannot be contained.

Jesus Christ offers forgiveness to the sinner because He came to save the lost of the world.

Jesus Christ will clothe His children in humility and will furnish us with great compassion.

Jesus Christ taught and lived kindness and gentleness because kind and gentle are two words which most accurately describe His character.

Jesus Christ, cause our faith to be as the faith of the Blessed Trinity's faith, and let our faithfulness to You be as Your faithfulness to our Father.

Jesus Christ, we love You and we thank You for Your great mercy which reaches from the farthest star of the north unto the farthest star of the south, and from the farthest star of the east unto the farthest star of the west.

Jesus Christ, cause us to walk in perfect unity, and cause us to love each other with the true love that You love us with.

Jesus Christ, cause the very steps of our thoughts to be under total submission and control of the Holy Ghost.

Jesus Christ, cause our ears to listen often and our lips to speak seldom.

Father God, thank You for the resurrection of Your precious Son Jesus Christ!

Jesus Christ, anoint these precious lambs with the spirit of evangelism.

Jesus Christ, seeking You is fun and has become our very reason for living.

Jesus Christ, let our lives be totally devoted to the diligent study of Your Word.

Jesus Christ, let our lives be invested in the helping of others through our prayers and with our money and time.

Jesus Christ, thank You for listening to and answering our prayers.

Jesus Christ, thank You for the gift of fasting.

Jesus Christ, teach us to love You and fear You as no other generation of Your people ever have.

Father God, thank You for the gift of the Holy Ghost.

In the name of the
Father, the Son and
the Holy Ghost

Amen and Amen
Copyright © 2008

30

Blessed of J.A.H.

A prayer of Mark Berryhill

JEHOVAH breathed life into Adam and JEHOVAH saw that His creation was good and that His called-out children would infinitely call unto Him as the LORD JEHOVAH.

JEHOVAH has a heart that is as delicate as the petals of beautiful roses which JEHOVAH himself creates, and the prayers of His saints are the pleasant fragrance which accompanies the same elegant white, red, orange and yellow roses created by the LORD JEHOVAH.

JEHOVAH and His innumerable company of angels are always prepared for peace and war, and JEHOVAH commands the armies of the angels of Heaven as compared to the display of the grace and beauty of a ballerina as she has just performed her greatest performance ever for her LORD JEHOVAH.

JEHOVAH sheds forth love, joy and goodness into the hearts of his children because within the heart of JEHOVAH love, joy and goodness ring out His own great name, the LORD GOD JEHOVAH!

JEHOVAH possesses great power because hell belongs to JEHOVAH, and yet His hearts desire is for each child to spend eternity with the Great LORD JEHOVAH!

JEHOVAH is love and love translated means JEHOVAH and His love can be neither contained on the earth nor in the Heaven which are both owned by the LORD JEHOVAH!

JEHOVAH and His children are one in JEHOVAH and the one true daddy of the human race is the LORD GOD JEHOVAH.

JEHOVAH walks in the oceans and rides on the clouds using the name J.A.H., because He is the Creator of the poets who with the gift of writing glorify the Father, the LORD GOD JEHOVAH!

JEHOVAH, You live in the very hearts of Your called-out children because LORD JEHOVAH, the only true good ever brought forth into this world is the precious lamb of our LORD GOD JEHOVAH!

JEHOVAH weeps and tears of joy run down His cheeks as do the great running rivers after the LORD JEHOVAH's down pours of rain and I hear Him softly whisper, My precious child, My love for these children can be neither weighed nor measured, it is immeasurable as I AM!

In the name of the
Father, the Son and
the Holy Ghost

Amen and Amen
Copyright © 2008

Beauty of Love II

A song of Mark Berryhill

Love is flowing from Heaven as do God's great rivers flow after His downpours of rain.

Love can be easily spoken and easily written but by the actions of people, motive of hearts are weighed.

Love and the true meaning of love was most accurately defined and demonstrated by a King who hung on the cross for His called-out children.

Love is the most powerful word known to mankind and love translated means JESUS CHRIST.

Love and the fulfillment thereof is why you and I came into existence and the reason the children are the great reward of the Almighty Father.

Love is proven by lending a hand to those in need while others pretend to not see the need of others.

Love is the reason God created the universe and the race referred to as mankind.

Love is demonstrated to others not by the mere speaking of the word; it is demonstrated by the true giving of ones heart to and for another person.

Love and its meaning is as the picture of a newly married couple who will ever presently have the cross of Christ before their spiritual eyes.

Love and the meaning of love is as the precious newborn baby girl who is being lovingly cradled by her mother for the first time.

Love is as James 1:27 states, "Pure religion and undefiled before God and the Father is this, to visit the fatherless and widows in their affliction, and to keep himself unspotted from the world."[2]

Love is the keeping of the commandments of our Almighty Father, and hearts motivated by love always outweigh following the letter of the law.

In the name of the
Father, the Son and
the Holy Ghost

Amen and Amen
Copyright © 2008

[2] James 1:27.

She will be Named Faith

A song of Mark Berryhill

Holy Ghost, thank You for living within the hearts of the Fathers called-out children.

Holy Ghost, thank You for the joy and comfort You bring into our hearts as we seek the Blessed Trinity.

Holy Ghost, may You become loved and adored as the Father and the Son are loved and adored!

Holy Ghost, may the world come to know the Father who never rests from caring for His called-out children.

Holy Ghost, may our lives and the lives of Your called-out children be invested in the diligent daily study of Your Word!

Holy Ghost, thank You for loving us as the Father and the Son love us.

Holy Ghost let the beauty of Your smile rest upon this beautiful nation known as the United States of America!

Holy Ghost, each day let the greatness of Your love be talked about from the opening of our eyes until the closing of our eyes.

Holy Ghost, let the joy and comfort that You bring into our lives be tasted by our precious lambs, days, months and years without end.

Holy Ghost, look at the beauty of the smile of the inquisitive precious baby girl clothed in the bright pink coat on this so very frigid day.

Holy Ghost, thank You for the spiritual growth we are enjoying in this blessed nation.

Holy Ghost may the brilliance of Your light shine majestically before the eyes of Your saints even unto the end of the world.

Holy Ghost, it is time for You, the Father, and the Son to go to work.

Holy Ghost, we love You, we adore You, we glorify You, and we need You in all that we do!

Holy Ghost, increase our faith and may You bless us with faith as faith as the Blessed Trinity's faith!

Holy Ghost, train our minds to walk in perfect precision and harmony with Your mind!

Holy Ghost, may knowing the Sword of the Spirit become the reason for the very existence of mankind.

Holy Ghost, cause the American Bald Eagle to soar on the wings of the angels of the Everlasting Father!

Holy Ghost, do You see the painting which reveals a baby girl who will be named Faith!

In the name of the
Father, the Son and
the Holy Ghost

Amen and Amen
Copyright © 2008

33

The Joy of Life

A song of Mark Berryhill

An increased faith in Christ and spiritual prosperity is the ultimate goal for each one of God's called-out children.

An increased love for the Father, the Holy Ghost and each other is the prayer of this blessed child of God.

An increased knowledge and understanding of God's Word will become the very reason for the existence of Christ's lambs.

An increased awareness of the constant spiritual needs of our precious lambs is a must in this generation where the most valuable commodity is time spent with Christ and His Word.

An increased awareness of the constant needs of orphans, and widows and the need of keeping oneself unspotted from the world.

An increased hope for the fulfillment of Christ's Great Commission.

An increased awareness of the comfort and joy shed forth into the hearts of God's children by the Holy Ghost.

An increased awareness to the world that the true ministers of Christ are the mothers, daddy's, teachers, principals and administrators who raise Christ's lambs in the daily admonition and nurture of the LORD.

An ever increasing realization of the beauty of God's creation and the ever present reality of the correct decision to serve Him whole heartedly and daily. An increased understanding of God's infinite love and faithfulness to His called-out children.

An increased awareness of the fact that for every action a reaction follows.

Holy Father, cause the motive and action of our hearts to be to feed Your precious lambs Your Word every day.

Holy Father, cause the world to know that the strength and wealth of our nation is YOU!

In the name of the
Father, the Son and
the Holy Ghost

Amen and Amen
Copyright © 2008

An Infinite Love

A prayer of Mark Berryhill

Jesus Christ is the King over this blessed nation we call the land of the free and home of the brave!

Jesus Christ is the ruler over the hearts and minds of His called-out children!

Jesus Christ, cause Your Spirit and song to dance in the hearts and minds of these precious lambs!

Jesus Christ, You will be exalted throughout the whole world as the one true King!

Jesus Christ, as Your rain is falling from Heaven this very day, so is Your faithfulness to Your called-out children!

Jesus Christ, so as the beauty of the varied colors in Your rainbow, so is the beauty of Your infinite love!

Jesus Christ, You are the friend and keeper of our souls because You and You alone are worthy to receive all of the glory, power, riches and honor!

Jesus Christ, thank You for the gift of our precious children!

Jesus Christ, thank You for molding us with Your skillful hands, as the potter who molds the clay!

Jesus Christ is love and there is no other who is loved and adored as is the King of kings and the Lord of lords!

Jesus Christ, bless the works of our hands and bless the works of our children's hands forevermore!

Jesus Christ, You will become the love and life of the American people!

Jesus Christ, thank You for the eternal victory You won for Your children at the cross known as Calvary!

Jesus Christ, thank You for friends who love You with all of their hearts, souls, minds and strength!

Jesus Christ, thank You for flowers which are clothed exquisitely in dresses of velvet!

Jesus Christ, You are a mystery and a friend, and the light which shines so magnificently and effortlessly in the hearts of Your precious lambs!

Jesus Christ, You my friend are the life, love and light of this beautiful creation known as the universe!

Jesus Christ, You and You alone are the great wealth of the United States of America!

In the name of the
Father, the Son and
the Holy Ghost

Amen and Amen
Copyright © 2008

35

Jesus Christ's Eternal Love

A prayer of Mark Berryhill

Love can melt hearts that are filled with anger, and nothing comforts hearts which have been hurt as does Jesus Christ's eternal love.

Love will change the world for Christ and nothing can comfort as does Jesus Christ's eternal love.

Love is knowing that you are saved because your Father created Jesus Christ's eternal love.

Love and mercy walk hand in hand as do the hands of a newly married couple who will forever be aware of Jesus Christ's eternal love.

Love and children are the Father's greatest gifts to His people, how could we ever question Jesus Christ's eternal love?

Love, parents, grandparents and the power of the Holy Ghost will open the world's eyes to Jesus Christ's eternal love.

Love is best described by the painting which reveals a mother holding her newborn son, and in her confidence knowing that he is protected by Jesus Christ's eternal love.

Love and faith are the two words which will cause the world to be set on fire by Jesus Christ's eternal love.

Love and joy can be compared to the beauty of God's creation as he begins to bloom this very season which also exquisitely demonstrates Jesus Christ's eternal love.

Love and faithfulness are the two words which best describe the character of our Father, and His proof is the victory won at the cross by Jesus Christ's eternal love.

Love is what is experienced by a mother as she watches her adorable daughter mature into a beautiful woman of God who is fully aware of Jesus Christ's eternal love.

Love is what is experienced by a father as he watches his precious son mature into a man with the mind of Christ who fully understands Jesus Christ's eternal love.

In the name of the
Father, the Son and
the Holy Ghost

Amen and Amen
Copyright © 2008

36

By the Love of Christ

A prayer of Mark Berryhill

How can men acquire the mind of Christ?

How will our every thought become the Word of God without intense daily memory work?

How will love ever be truly perfected if we do not learn how to give our lives for the other person?

How will Christ's children conquer the world without total submission to the Holy Spirit?

How will hearts that are filled with pain be changed into hearts that are filled with joy?

How can wisdom be acquired without diligently studying the book which was written by the Creator of wisdom?

How will a young man know the difference between good and evil without having the Sword of the Spirit written onto his heart?

How will a person know that true joy comes from freely giving one's heart for the other person?

How can we fully enjoy life without constantly praying?

How can the American Bald Eagle soar on the wings of the angels of the Everlasting Father without diligent fasting by the American people?

How can we say I love you and not lend our heart when the other person is in need of a true friend?

How can we fully comprehend love without having the cross of Christ ever presently before our spiritual eyes?

In the name of the
Father, the Son and
the Holy Ghost

Amen and Amen
Copyright © 2008

Father, Son and Holy Ghost

A song of Mark Berryhill

God causes joy to overflow in the hearts of His children, and the laughter of children brings joy into the heart of God.

God is love and He came to seek and save the lost because a pure and perfect heart is the heart within our Father God.

God created the beauty of the universe in six days and rested on the seventh day, His omniscient presence and unmatched power are just two reasons to call the LORD your God.

God created the love that exists within His children, and there is no other who deserves all of the praise, glory, honor and power as does the Almighty God.

God blesses and blesses and blesses because it is better to give than to receive, and for Him to have one more precious child praying unto Him makes His heart leap with joy, He is God.

God desires for us to be happy and filled with joy, and the true joy of living is found in diligently and daily seeking the face of JESUS.

God the Father, the Lord Jesus Christ, the Holy Ghost and the Word will become engrained into the very hearts and minds of the children of God.

God offers eternal life to the people of the world through the blood of a precious lamb that was found without blemish because true love was created by JEHOVAH.

The vision reveals Christ standing on the earth with outstretched arms, and as His head is tilted upward toward Heaven, He prays without ceasing for each child of the Most High God.

Christ's universe and the brilliance thereof manifests His glory, and yet the gifts of love and children are the greatest gifts of JESUS CHRIST!

In the name of the
Father, the Son and
the Holy Ghost

Amen and Amen
Copyright © 2008

Love and Unity

A song of Mark Berryhill

How much does Jesus Christ love you?

Are you truly willing to lay down your life for your brother?

Will you and I obey the words which are written in the Gospel of Jesus Christ?

When the King knocks on your door and asks for you to do a favor for Him, will you obey His voice or pretend as if you didn't hear Him?

The beauty of the lake brings joy into our hearts, and the singing of the birds offers a new melody to our ears.

The guitarist strums his guitar with precision and the song he sings about JESUS echoes through the canyons of the same lake, and causes the waves to suddenly appear as if they are dancing.

The beginning of summer sheds forth and intensifies the beauty of God's cities throughout this great country known as the United States of America.

Old leaves have recently fallen from the last freeze and life now blossoms forth before our appreciate eyes.

The aroma and beauty of God's roses share a small glimpse of what paradise with our Father will be like.

The vision reveals precious young girls clothed in dresses of beauty, they are dancing in perfect unison and their song flows even through the distant mountains.

The words of their song resounds, JESUS, we love You, JESUS, we need You, JESUS, You are our joy and our hope.

The vision reveals young boys clothed in khaki pants, blue button down shirts, and nicely designed matching shoes.

They are singing in perfect unison and their words also flow through distant mountains, JESUS, we love You, JESUS, we need You, JESUS, You are our joy and our hope.

God blesses love and unity, and helping other people to manifest their talents is great joy.

In the name of the
Father, the Son and
the Holy Ghost

Amen and Amen
Copyright © 2008

A Perfect Heart II

A song of Mark Berryhill

Jesus is the light of the world, and He always will be.

Jesus is the love in your heart, and He always will be.

Jesus is the King of kings and the Lord of lords, and He always will be.

Jesus is the breath of life, and He always will be.

Jesus is faithful and He always will be.

Jesus is the ruler over Heaven and earth, and He always will be.

Jesus is love, light and life, and He always will be.

All praise, glory and honor to God the Father, the Lord Jesus Christ, and the Holy Ghost.

In the name of the
Father, the Son and
the Holy Ghost

Amen and Amen
Copyright © 2008

Messiah

By Mark Berryhill

A Tear of Joy

A prayer of Mark Berryhill

Holy Ghost, thank You for living within the hearts and minds of the children of Jesus Christ!

Holy Ghost, thank You for the joy and comfort that You bring into the hearts of the children of Jesus Christ!

Holy Ghost, thank You for life and thank You for the great victory won because of the blood of Jesus Christ!

Holy Ghost, thank You for the love and power that You bring into the hearts of the children of Jesus Christ!

Holy Ghost, we want to sing and dance and tell You that we love You as we love Jesus Christ!

Holy Ghost, may our children be made to know Your great faithfulness, and the infinite love of Jesus Christ!

Holy Ghost, let us not love one another in word only, but let us love one another with the true love of Jesus Christ!

Holy Ghost, let forgiveness always be readily found in our hearts as it is with our Lord Jesus Christ!

Holy Ghost, reach down from Heaven and place these precious lambs into the heart of our King, Jesus Christ!

Holy Ghost, let peace and prosperity flourish throughout the United States of America, and may the hearts and minds of these precious lambs be the dwelling place of Jesus Christ!

Holy Ghost, we love You, and we adore You, come heal our land because of the beauty of the prayer of an adorable four year old baby girl.

Holy Ghost, by Your power set an erring world back onto the pathway of righteousness and holiness for Jesus Christ!

Holy Ghost, life is wonderful because of You!

In the name of the
Father, the Son and
the Holy Ghost

Amen and Amen
Copyright © 2008

The Beauty of Christ

A song of Mark Berryhill

The beauty Jesus brings into the everyday lives of His people is as a painting the brilliant artist has just completed by bringing to life the rising of the majestic sun! The beauty Jesus brings into the hearts of His children is as the rapid flowing river as it races from the tallest of snow capped mountains to the lowest of the valleys! The beauty Jesus offers His most recent convert is a life full of joy, and an eternity spent with the Blessed Trinity in paradise!

The beauty Jesus causes our hearts to know because of His eternal care is as the painting of a young boy softly calling unto His daddy whom he knows will always be there for him!

The beauty Jesus causes His children to know in their hearts is as the picture of sky reaching mountains of the far north, and of the beautiful and varied types of wild animals of God's creative creation!

The beauty Jesus sheds forth into the hearts of His children is as the joy a young man and young woman experience as they say "I do" and kiss!

The beauty Jesus causes in the hearts of His children is most magnificently demonstrated by the beautiful babies brought forth from the union of faithful mothers and daddies who said "I do."

The beauty Jesus brings into the hearts of His children is as the painting in which the cheetah effortlessly out runs the storm that is seemingly pursuing her!

The beauty Jesus brings into our hearts is as the rain from Heaven which produces the food for these precious babies!

The beauty Jesus brings into our lives is as a picture of the refuge which is provided for the seemingly helpless and hopeless!

The beauty Jesus brings into the hearts of His children is as the picture of a great herd of elephants moving from their old location to their new location!

The beauty of Jesus is as the painting of the American Bald Eagle as he soars on the wings of the angels of the Everlasting Father!

The beauty of Jesus is as the painting that reveals a mother as she gently cradles her newborn baby girl for the first time!

In the name of the
Father, the Son and
the Holy Ghost

Amen and Amen
Copyright © 2008

Messiah

A prayer of Mark Berryhill

Messiah sits on the throne because He obeyed His Father's voice and laid down His life for the ones He loves.

Messiah utters His voice and the Heavens shutter as when the wind of the hurricane of destruction makes his way to an isolated island.

Messiah is King because his love for you reaches from everlasting to everlasting.

Messiah makes prayers a reality because His Spirit leads the prayers of His children.

Messiah clothes the flowers in dresses of velvet, and forms these precious babies in the wombs of their mothers with His skillful and yet delicate hands.

Messiah causes dolphins to soar through the air with grace and ease, and His teachings will control the world forevermore.

Messiah watches over the cattle of the north, south, east and west, and He caused our dinner plates to overflow for days without end because of His enduring goodness.

Messiah softly whispers to me and says, "The love I possess for these precious children can be neither weighed nor measured, it is immeasurable."

Messiah is filled with joy when His lambs are fed His Word daily, and He is filled with anger when they are not.

Messiah sheds forth love and grace into the hearts of His children because His love and His grace for His called-out children is infinite.

Messiah spoke seldom because the Holy Ghost and wisdom dwelt with Him, and His words are the words of eternal life.

Messiah can take the worst of sinners and make them His shinning stars.

Messiah can take hearts that are broken and turn them into hearts of gold and hearts of silver.

In the name of the
Father, the Son and
the Holy Ghost

Amen and Amen
Copyright © 2008

Dresses of Velvet

A prayer of Mark Berryhill

The wife is on a short journey and while she is away, her husband prepares gardens of flowers for her return.

The flowers are beautiful and clothed in velvet dresses of different colors.

As we look upon the brilliant colors of the flowers, joy is shed forth into our hearts by their overwhelming beauty.

The husband toils for the duration of the day, diligently arranging the flowers for his wife's return.

To see the joy expressed by the man's wife as she returned and saw the flowers made my heart leap with joy.

Father, thank You for being a God of romance.

Father, thank You for husbands and wives who continue to be in love with each other after twenty years of faithful marriage.

Father, thank You for husbands who love their wives, and for wives who love their husbands as You love Your called-out children.

Lord Jesus, thank You for the beauty of recently born puppies that make our days just a little bit brighter.

Father, thank You for pine trees that reach into Heaven and sing songs of beauty as we walk by them.

Father, thank You for life and for the joy that living for You brings into our hearts.

In the name of the
Father, the Son and
the Holy Ghost

Amen and Amen
Copyright © 2008

One Nation under God

A song of Mark Berryhill

God blesses unity, and spiritual gifts are manifested because of obedience to His Word and His voice.

God is to be exalted by everyone because He is the Creator of all things.

God is to be loved and adored because our sins were nailed to the cross with His precious Son.

God is sovereign, and for Him to transform our schools into the greatest daily training facilities of His Word is as simple for Him as to speak and create light.

God is love, and for Him to transform the nations of the world into the United States of America is a worthy goal.

God desires for our children to become great men and women of faith, therefore their hearts must be nurtured daily with His Word.

God's enemy came to kill, steal and destroy, and yet by the power of the Holy Ghost we will protect Christ's lambs from being devoured by the subtlety of the enemy.

God rides on the clouds, and walks in the oceans using the name J.A.H.

God is the Creator and sustainer of life and through faith in the blood of His Son, there is eternal life.

God the Father, the Lord Jesus Christ, and the Holy Ghost are victorious. Follow the righteous pathway of the Trinity.

God is pleased with those who exalt and obey Him, and He is filled with wrath against the non-believers of this world.

God is but a prayer away, if you are in need, call unto Him and before you finish praying, He will be there with you.

God is a God of hope, and for Him nothing is impossible.

In the name of the
Father, the Son and
the Holy Ghost

Amen and Amen
Copyright © 2008

A Cross of Love

A song of Mark Berryhill

Love causes a young man's heart to race as his future bride walks into the room, and yet the bride's heart races as does his because she also is in love.

Love brings sinners to the foot of the cross, and Jesus Christ can be likewise spelled love.

Love is meant to be for eternity, and the proof of our Father's goodness is Jesus Christ's victory at the cross of love.

Love causes the twinkle in our own eyes as we see our baby boys and baby girls begin opening their Christmas presents once again, and experience that giving brings forth love.

Love is defined by parents who understand the importance of feeding Christ's lambs in our public schools daily, and faith in Christ is produced in us by His love.

Love causes young lovers to see stars as they kiss, and precious newborn baby girls and baby boys are the result of love.

Faith in Jesus comes from the Holy Ghost, and through the diligent study of God's Word love begins walking hand in hand with faith.

Faith is passed down to children from parents of faith, and yet the grandparents also play such a vital role in the continuation of faith.

Faith in Jesus Christ causes our hearts to dance, and the joy His love and faithfulness brings into our lives creates even more faith.

Hope is shed forth into our hearts because of the love of a precious lamb that was found without blemish. Jesus Christ is the Creator of hope.

Hope is brought forth to the ears of stranded and near dead people of a shipwreck as they hear the rescue helicopters finally approaching; they now understand the definition of hope.

Hope is a word of beauty, and beauty is created by hope.

In the name of the
Father, the Son and
the Holy Ghost

Amen and Amen
Copyright © 2008

Love, Faith, Hope

A song of Mark Berryhill

Love reigns within the heart of our Father, and His grace blossoms forth throughout America as His smile rests upon this great land.

Love is the reason that our Father created the universe, and also the reason why He sent His precious Son Jesus.

Love is the reason a precious and adorable newborn baby girl takes her first look at light as she departs her ready mother's body.

Love is turning the other cheek when retaliation would seem as the appropriate action to be taken.

Love is forgiving the other person when the other person asks to be forgiven, and even when they don't.

God is love and His love will never be taken from you because of His great faithfulness.

Love causes newlyweds to dance under the moonlight even until the rising of God's sun.

Love says yes to good and goodness, and no to evil.

Love is so accurately demonstrated by the painting which reveals the great grandmother as she rocks on the porch of her 100 year old farm house with God's Word grasped ever so tightly in her hands.

Faith in Christ and in His power is how the world will be won for Him.

Faith makes us to know that our Father will never leave nor forsake us.

Faith in Christ places confidence and love into the hearts of His children, and turns frowning faces into smiling faces.

Hope is what is sent forth to the people who have found themselves in seeming hopeless situations.

Hope, and the guarantee thereof, is given to Christ's children because of His great faithfulness at His cross.

Hope is given by God's children to the less fortunate of the world as His Word is spread throughout the world.

Hope is a word of beauty that creates beauty in the very hearts of its readers.

Hope, and our faith in Jesus Christ, will win the world for Him, and as is the painting of a little boy who has both arms lifted high in a confirming sign of His confidence in his Christ.

In the name of the
Father, the Son and
the Holy Ghost

Amen and Amen
Copyright © 2008

A Tender Heart

A song of Mark Berryhill

Have you considered how beautiful the smile of a precious daughter truly is?
Have you considered the tender heart that resides within the precious Son?
Have you considered how much love God bestowed upon mankind at the cross of His Son?
Have you considered how beautiful life truly is?
Have you considered how much energy God exerts for the human race to exist each day?
Have you considered that without God as our focus life is meaningless?
Have you considered that with God as our focus, living is a joy surpassed by no other?
Have you considered that the reason for our existence is to feed Christ's lambs daily?
Have you considered how much God loves you?
Have you considered that God willingly offered His precious Son for you and your sins because of His enormous and infinite love for you?
Have you considered how wonderful it is to watch God's sun rise this very morning?
Have you considered that by the power of Christ's love, and by your faith in Him, you can win the world for Him?
Have you considered that prosperity is to love your Father with all of your heart, soul, mind and strength?
Have you considered that prosperity is to love your neighbor as you love yourself?
Have you considered the beauty of God's sun as he sets today?
Have you considered that love and life were created by a genius who goes by the name El Shaddai?

In the name of the
Father, the Son and
the Holy Ghost

Amen and Amen
Copyright © 2008

God is Love II

A song of Mark Berryhill

The love the Almighty possesses for you can be neither weighed nor measured, it is immeasurable!

The love that God bestowed upon mankind at His cross can not be expressed with even the most brilliant of words known to the human race!

Let no man or woman resist the love that Christ has bestowed upon them!

God's love is not a love that is taken away, His love is a love that grows even stronger as we draw nearer to Him!

Father, my prayer is that these precious children in this nation and throughout the world will be taught by Your Spirit to truly love You with every fiber of their being!

Father, continue to let Your smile rest upon this great land, and cause Your wisdom and knowledge to be shed forth into the hearts of these precious lambs.

Father, raise up laborers for the harvest, for the laborers are few but the harvest is great.

Father, thank You for kittens which show us how tender our children's hearts are as they gently cuddle them.

Father, bless these precious lambs with Your love and with Your grace, cause their days to be invested in the diligent daily study of Your Word.

Father, we love You, we need You, we adore You, and we glorify You!

Father, as the lake cools and refreshes us on a hot summer day, so let Your Spirit refresh the hearts and minds of Your children.

Father, thank You for the gift of life, and for the gift of love.

Father, thank You for the two precious newborn babies who were just shown to me.

Father, thank You for the love and goodness that our children bring into our hearts.

Father, I see the blood as it pours from the thorns which are placed in the head of Your precious Son, and I say, "Why my Lord?"

Father, thank You for the blood of Your precious lamb which covers the sins for Your children throughout infinite!

Father, thank You for the greatest victory that will ever be known to the human race, the love shed forth by JESUS CHRIST at His cross!

In the name of the
Father, the Son and
the Holy Ghost

Amen and Amen
Copyright © 2008

An Infinite Love

A prayer of Mark Berryhill

Father, thank You for the free gift of grace You extend to Your children because of Your Son's obedience at His cross.

Father, thank You for the free gift of our precious children.

Father, mold us with Your skillful hands and cause our days to be invested in diligent daily study of Your Word.

Father, thank You for the married men and women who have been faithful to You and to the vows they confessed before You.

Father, thank You for parents and grandparents who have their children in church worshipping You at every possible opportunity.

Father, by Your love, by Your power, and by Your Spirit, please transform our public schools into the greatest daily training facilities of Your Word that there has ever been.

Father, cause Your love to flow from Heaven, even as Your rivers flow after Your great down pours of rain.

Father, thank You for our baby boys who say prayers unto You that are so beautiful that our hearts and lives will be changed forever.

Father, thank You for our baby girls who can recite the twenty-third Psalms from memory which causes Your heart to be filled with joy.

Father, thank You for love and life.

Father, teach us to love You with all of our hearts, souls, minds and strength.

Father, cause our hearts to be filled with Your love, and may You anoint us and our children with the Spirit and gift of evangelism.

Father, teach us how to truly forgive one another.

Father, walk these precious children in the pathway of righteousness for Your great names sake!

Father, we love You, we adore You, we need You and we exalt You!

All praise, glory, honor and power to God the Father, the Lord Jesus Christ and the Holy Ghost!

In the name of the
Father, the Son and
the Holy Ghost

Amen and Amen
Copyright © 2008

Children of Faith II

A prayer of Mark Berryhill

Holy Ghost, cause Your indescribable love to be felt throughout the earth in its entirety!

Holy Ghost, shower Your love down from Heaven even as Your great downpours of rain.

Holy Ghost, we pray that You will make the hearts and minds of our children Your dwelling place!

Holy Ghost, cause the sad to be made happy.

Holy Ghost, thank You for the beauty caused by Your most recent showers of rain.

Holy Ghost, let love and forgiveness be the pathways that Your people choose to walk in.

Holy Ghost, thank You for the Spiritual and physical health that we are enjoying today.

Holy Ghost, thank You for the blood of a precious lamb that was found without blemish!

Holy Ghost, thank You for mothers who love their children with all of their hearts, souls, minds and strength!

Holy Ghost, thank You for our children that bring such goodness and joy into our hearts!

Holy Ghost, cause Your people to understand the importance of being fruitful and multiplying in order to raise children of faith!

Holy Ghost, thank You for faithful fathers who love their children with all of their hearts, souls, minds and strength.

Holy Ghost, as the beauty of snow-capped mountains shed forth such great beauty to our eyes, so let the beauty and goodness of Your heart rest upon this great land known as the United States of America!

Holy Ghost, may You, the Father, and the Son be loved, adored and exalted by all of Your people.

Holy Ghost let the love of the Blessed Trinity be written in the hearts of this great generation of people that You have created.

Holy Ghost, we love You, we need You, we adore You, we exalt You, and we want our babies to do likewise.

Holy Ghost, bless our children with faith as the Blessed Trinity's faith!

In the name of the
Father, the Son and
the Holy Ghost

Amen and Amen
Copyright © 2008

A Dance with Love

A prayer of Mark Berryhill

Father, thank You for the gift of life!

Father, thank You for Your free gift of eternal grace!

Father, thank You for loving Your children beyond what the human mind can comprehend!

Father, thank You for the rain You poured on this little city the very day I write these words of thanksgiving and inspiration!

Father, thank You for the gifts of love and forgiveness.

Father, teach us to truly love You with all of our hearts, souls, minds and strength!

Father, teach us to truly love our neighbors as we love ourselves!

Father, as the beautifully sculptured trees seem to dance as Your wind gusts around them, so let our days be spent singing and dancing before You!

Father, thank You for the gift of marriage!

Father, help us be good parents to our children, and good sons and daughters unto You!

Father, thank You, thank You, thank You!

Father, thank You for being able to carry the world by the great and exceeding power of Your right hand!

Father, all praise, glory, honor, and power belong to You; Your Son and Your Spirit, for You truly are the Great I AM!

In the name of the
Father, the Son and
the Holy Ghost

Amen and Amen
Copyright © 2008

God with Us II

A song of Mark Berryhill

Jesus causes our hearts to be filled with joy and goodness, and the most wonderful name in the human language is Jesus.

Jesus creates these precious and beautiful children in the wombs of their mothers with His skillful and delicate hands because love translated means Jesus.

Jesus causes the flowers to bloom with colors of brilliance, and makes the dry and barren land to bring forth food for His children because no one loves His children as does King Jesus.

Jesus, we love You, we adore You, and we need You, may You become the very reason for the existence of Your children Lord Jesus.

Jesus, thank You for nice homes, nice vehicles, and plenty of food, cause our eyes to be totally focused on serving You Lord Jesus.

Jesus, thank You for the free gift of Your eternal grace, and for the precious and appreciated gift of our lambs Lord Jesus.

Jesus, thank You for Your faithfulness and for Your unfailing love, Immanuel.

Jesus, thank You for the sun, moon and the brilliant racing stars; thank You for day and for night, Prince of Peace.

Jesus, as the baby birds crave the attention and nurturing of their mother, so may our children crave Your Word days, months and years without end, Wonderful Counselor.

Jesus, thank You for green pastures covered with morning dew and thank You for the gift of intimacy between husbands and wives, Creator of life.

Jesus, bless the works of our children's hands forevermore, and may You be glorified in the days of new, even as in the days of old, I AM THAT I AM.

In the name of the
Father, the Son and
the Holy Ghost

Amen and Amen
Copyright © 2008

Laughter of a Child

A prayer of Mark Berryhill

Holy Ghost, life is precious, and the gift and beauty of children brings joy and goodness into our hearts.

Holy Ghost, according to Your Word, for us to love You and each other is the fulfilling of Your law.

Holy Ghost, in life there are difficulties and obstacles, and yet by our faith in You we will overcome the world for Christ.

Holy Ghost let the children of the world be the apple of Your eye.

Holy Ghost, may You become loved and adored even as the Father and the Son are loved and adored.

Holy Ghost, thank You for rain and food.

Holy Ghost, thank You for Your great faithfulness!

Holy Ghost, as the sound of racing rivers, after one of God's downpours of rain, so let Your Word and voice be our guide.

Holy Ghost, train our spiritual ears to discern Your voice even as our King while

He was here on this beautiful land known as earth.

Holy Ghost, thank You for living within Your called-out children, and thank You for cool mornings, hot days and cool nights.

Holy Ghost, thank You for this blessed nation known as the United States of America.

Holy Ghost let the laughter of Your children resound through the Heavens, and let heir smiles be ever-presently placed before the Father of lights.

Holy Ghost, You are great!

Holy Ghost, teach us Your ways, and may You become the delight of the hearts of Your called-out children.

Holy Ghost, let love reign in the hearts and minds of Jesus Christ's lambs!

Holy Ghost, let our every breath be to praise You, and may the reason for our existence be to spread the Word of God!

In the name of the
Father, the Son and
the Holy Ghost

Amen and Amen
Copyright © 2008

The Love of Christ

A prayer of Mark Berryhill

He offers eternal salvation to His beloved because He is the Creator of love and life.

He desires a people that will give their hearts to Him and their lives for Him.

He loves you more than He loves His universe because you, my precious child, were made and created in His image.

He offers hope to the hopeless and eternal life unto the eternally damned.

He desires for His children to enjoy the gift of life.

He created faith in the faithless by their diligent study of His Word, and places love into hearts that are filled with hate.

He and His Word offer love, life, light and hope for His called-out children, and He is our future.

He causes His magnificent sun to rise each morning, and His sun to set each day, and by His sun warmth and goodness is provided unto the world.

He causes the moon to glisten and shed forth light during the comforting hours of the night.

He is the Creator of all good things, may we learn to love Him with every beat of our hearts.

He is the Alpha and the Omega; and in His right hand is the very breath of our lives.

Jesus, teach us to love You with every fiber of our existence.

Jesus, fill our children with Your love, Your knowledge, and Your Spirit.

All praise, glory, honor and power to God the Father, the Lord Jesus Christ, and the Holy Ghost.

My dear friends look at the beauty and awesomeness of our LORD's creation which surrounds us, and we know that love translated is JESUS.

The blood of the child brought forth by the beloved Mary is the reason for the birth of each of His beloved children.

The American Bald Eagle soars on the wings of the angels of the Everlasting Father!

In the name of the
Father, the Son and
the Holy Ghost

Amen and Amen
Copyright © 2008

57

A Rose and a Cross

A song of Mark Berryhill

Love is the most beautiful word of any language, and mountains which seem unmovable to the natural eye can easily be moved with love.

Love is a word that will change the world for Jesus Christ and His character and demonstration of His unfathomable love for you was best displayed at His cross of love.

Love is a word that paints a picture which reveals a wooden cross, and on that cross there hangs a beautiful red rose which signifies the eternal beauty of the blood of Immanuel's love.

Love reveals a world filled with precious daughters and wonderful sons which are free gifts from the Creator of love.

Love flows down from Heaven from the Father of lights, and our hearts are filled with quality of life and His infinite love.

Love is so accurately demonstrated by the artist who has captured the scene of a mother as she gently hugs her precious son, and rocks him in a chair that has been past down through the years by other mothers who also understood that a child and a mothers love for her child is from the God of love.

Love forgives while hate seeks revenge, and love exhorts and comforts while hate tears down.

Love carries the other person when the other person can not carry themselves, and hate pretends not to see the needs of others.

Love and the definition thereof is the diligent teaching of God's Word in the daily lives of His lambs.

Love and the innocent lamb found without blemish has changed the world forevermore.

The brilliant artists painting reveals our King on His cross of love, His blood is flowing from the crown of thorns placed within His head, a gentle falling tear runs down my cheek, and I say, oh my Lord, oh that I could have died for You!

In the name of the
Father, the Son and
the Holy Ghost

Amen and Amen
Copyright © 2008

58

Love, Mercy and Peace

A song of Mark Berryhill

Holy Ghost, thank You for dwelling within the hearts of Jesus Christ's lambs.
Holy Ghost, thank You for the gift of adorable daughters and wonderful sons.
Holy Ghost, let Your love flow down from Heaven, and cause Your children to understand the beauty of living.
Holy Ghost, we praise You, we glorify You, we need You and we love You!
Holy Ghost, let love, mercy and peace reign in the lives of Jesus Christ's lambs.
Holy Ghost let the focus of our lives be to serve You with pure and perfect hearts.
Holy Ghost, thank You for causing Your called-out children to love You with all of our hearts, souls, minds and strength.
Holy Ghost, You are the reason for the joy in our hearts today, therefore, let our song be to please You today, and for all of the tomorrows.
Holy Ghost, great dark overshadowing clouds reveal a glimpse of the strength of our Almighty Father's right arm, and the birth of newborn children are His great reward.
Holy Ghost, trees of beauty appear to dance as Your wind gusts around them and the life and light of men is Jesus Christ.
Holy Ghost let the Spirit of evangelism be poured upon Your children, and let our lives be invested in the diligent daily study of Your Word.
Holy Ghost, all praise, glory, honor and power belong to the Father, the Son and You, for You truly are the great I AM!

In the name of the
Father, the Son and
the Holy Ghost

Amen and Amen
Copyright © 2008

59

Abba, Abba

A song of Mark Berryhill

JEHOVAH creates these precious and delicate children, how could you ever question His unfathomable love for you?

J.A.H. rides on the clouds, and walks in the waters of the deep because He is able.

El Shaddai saved Isaac from Abraham's knife because of His infinite wisdom.

Adonai sings with a voice which roars as does a lion, even the Lion of Judah.

Elohim dances in the heaven of heavens each time one of these precious lambs accepts the King as their personal Savior.

Alpha and Omega resound throughout the Heavens, and the earth will dissolve soon after Omega follows Alpha!

I AM THAT I AM rules in Heaven and on earth, for everything in Heaven and earth belongs to I AM!

The Prince of Peace sheds forth peace into the very lives of His called-out children, and nothing can separate you from His infinite love for you!

Can you hear the voices of the angels as they sing together in perfect unison and harmony to bring glory to the GOD of all?

The Wonderful Counselor is but a heart beat and prayer away, if you find yourself desiring to serve Him with every fiber of your existence!

The Mighty God is victorious, walk with Him, for to be separated from Him is to be in an eternal fire without hope!

JESUS CHRIST is the King of kings and Lord of lords because His Father is Abba, Abba.

In the name of the
Father, the Son and
the Holy Ghost

Amen and Amen
Copyright © 2008

Immanuel's Love

A prayer of Mark Berryhill

Father, thank You for the gift of life!

Father, thank You for your unfathomable gift of love displayed at the cross of Your precious Son, Immanuel!

Father, thank You for Your grace which will carry the souls of Your called-out children throughout infinity!

Father, thank You for our sons, and for our daughters!

Father, thank You for the breath of life and for the place we will lay our tired heads this very night!

Father, bless Your called-out children with faith as the Blessed Trinity's faith!

Father, shower Your love, wisdom, knowledge, and understanding upon Your lambs!

Father, thank You for the beauty of the smiles of children, and for the goodness that resides within their hearts!

Father, with the invisible ink of Your pen, write Your Word on the hearts and minds of Your children!

Father, thank You for faithful priests, and thank You for Your love which will never be taken away from Your called-out children!

Father, Your Holy Spirit causes our hearts to leap with joy, and we crave Your Word as our food more than food itself!

Eternal Father, thank You, thank You, thank You for the eternal victory brought forth by the blood of Your Son, Immanuel!

In the name of the
Father, the Son and
the Holy Ghost

Amen and Amen
Copyright © 2008

61

Christ's Crown of Glory

A prayer of Mark Berryhill

The painting reveals an undeserved crown of thorns that is placed around the King's head, His blood gently pours down His face, and I ask Him, why my LORD?

The artist's brilliant painting of the King hanging on the cross turns a gentle falling tear into a flowing river of tears.

With outstretched arms, and with nails placed within His delicate hands and feet, the artist has captured the essence of the love of Jesus Christ, "Greater love hath no man than this that a man lay down his life for his friends."[3]

The cross of Jesus Christ was and always will be the greatest victory ever won for God's called-out children.

The blood of Jesus Christ redeemed the Father's children back unto Him.

There is great power in the blood of the Lamb that was found without blemish, His blood offers forth Your eternal salvation.

JESUS CHRIST is the very reason for the creation of life!

In the name of the
Father, the Son and
the Holy Ghost

Amen and Amen
Copyright © 2008

[3] John 15:13.

The Power of Vision

A song of Mark Berryhill

In the right hand of the eleven year old boy as he enters his school house is a book which is covered in a black leather cover, the books name is the Holy Bible.

The boy's school house will become another place where the young boy is both taught his Father's Word and filled with his Father's Spirit.

In the right hand of the nine year old girl as she enters the school house is a book which is covered in a black leather cover, the book's name is God's Sword of the Spirit.

The young girl's school house will become another place where the young girl is both taught her Father's Word and filled with her Father's Spirit.

JEHOVAH, may You be loved, adored and glorified by our children today and always!

The American Bald Eagle soars on the wings of the angels of the Everlasting Father!

In the name of the
Father, the Son and
the Holy Ghost

Amen and Amen
Copyright © 2008

JESUS is Life

A song of Mark Berryhill

Holy Ghost, thank You for the blessing of love.

Holy Ghost, thank You for writing our Father's Word onto our hearts, and onto our children's hearts.

Holy Ghost, teach us to lay down our lives for You by being totally submitted to Your lead.

Holy Ghost, thank You for the beauty of the creation, and for the gift of life.

In the name of the
Father, the Son and
the Holy Ghost

Amen and Amen
Copyright © 2008

Eternal Father

A prayer of Mark Berryhill

Eternal Father, cause love, joy, peace, longsuffering, gentleness, goodness, faith, meekness and temperance to reign in our hearts.

Eternal Father, cause us to be set apart for You and consecrated to You.

Eternal Father, anoint us with the Spirit of evangelism so that we will boldly proclaim Your Word throughout the world.

Eternal Father, walk us in the pathway of obedience today and for all of the tomorrows.

In the name of the
Father, the Son and
the Holy Ghost

Amen and Amen
Copyright © 2008

Father, Son and Holy Ghost

A prayer of Mark Berryhill

Holy Ghost, teach us to walk in Your power, with Your confidence, and by Your faith.

Holy Ghost, teach us to enjoy the beauty of life, and we thank You for the breath of life.

Holy Ghost, transform our nation into a nation of people that seek You every moment of every day.

In the name of the
Father, the Son and
the Holy Ghost

Amen and Amen
Copyright © 2008

God of Victory

A prayer of Mark Berryhill

Lord Jesus, we love You, we praise You, and we glorify You and we thank You for the beauty of Your magnificent creation.

Lord Jesus, we thank You for the rain which makes Your earth so fresh and clean.

Lord Jesus, I thank You for the unfathomable love You displayed for Your people at the cross of victory!

Father, thank You for the blood of the precious lamb that was found without blemish.

In the name of the
Father, the Son and
the Holy Ghost

Amen and Amen
Copyright © 2008

Love and Grace

A song of Mark Berryhill

Can the love that a mother possesses for her newborn baby girl be either weighed or measured?
Can the love that a father possesses for his newborn son be either weighed or measured?
Consider the great love parents have for their children, and yet the love Jesus Christ bestowed upon you at His cross is exceedingly greater!
Jesus Christ endured the pain of the cross for you because He understands the meanings of love and grace.

In the name of the
Father, the Son and
the Holy Ghost

Amen and Amen
Copyright © 2008

Lamb of God

A song of Mark Berryhill

God's golden sun presents a radiant smile, and joy enters into the hearts of the little ones, while the gentleness of God's moon tells a story of the gentleness of God's character.

Beautifully designed crosses and elegantly arranged flowers unite and rejoice by singing a song of victory about Jesus and His cross at the graves of His beloved. Blood pours from the thorns that are placed within our Lord's precious head, and tears begin once again to run down my cheeks; I then suddenly realize that because of God's infinite love, and because of the power of the blood of the Lamb, we have eternal life.

In the name of the
Father, the Son and
the Holy Ghost

Amen and Amen
Copyright © 2008

Heart of our Father

A song of Mark Berryhill

Holy Father, please cause the Christians to rise up and fulfill Your hearts desire by evangelizing the world with Your Word.

Holy Father, walk us in the light of Your Son Jesus today, and for all of the tomorrows.

Holy Father, let the beauty and radiance of Your majestic smile rest upon this beautiful planet named earth.

Holy Father, thank You!

In the name of the
Father, the Son and
the Holy Ghost

Amen and Amen
Copyright © 2008

Christ is the Gift

A song of Mark Berryhill

Jesus Christ creates the beauty that each day brings forth.

Jesus Christ forms these precious, adorable and helpless babies in the wombs of their mothers because He is the great I AM!

Jesus Christ gave His life for you because His love for You exceeds even the distance it is from the farthest star of the west unto the farthest star of the east.

Simple, Jesus Christ is love, and the laughter of His children causes His heart to leap with joy!

In the name of the
Father, the Son and
the Holy Ghost

Amen and Amen
Copyright © 2008

Christ Reigns

A song of Mark Berryhill

His smile appears to be dancing, while His heart of gold leaps with joy.
His love for His children surpasses even the distance it is to the farthest star
of the north, which He Himself placed with His delicate yet strong fingers.
His Spirit is the life and light of His called-out children, and the beauty of His
unfathomable greatness!
His name rings forth throughout the Heavens; listen as the angels sing in
perfect unison and harmony, Immanuel!

In the name of the
Father, the Son and
the Holy Ghost

Amen and Amen
Copyright © 2008

The Most Perfect Gifts

A song of Mark Berryhill

Offer a prayer of thanksgiving unto our God because He has truly blessed us with the most perfect gifts!

He is great, and He and He alone is worthy to receive all of the praise, glory and honor!

J.A.H. is His name and the clouds are His chariot.

Father, cause Your children to multiply, and to become innumerable, even as the stars of Heaven, which are innumerable.

Father, thank You for our precious children, and for Immanuel, the most perfect gifts!

In the name of the
Father, the Son and
the Holy Ghost

Amen and Amen
Copyright © 2008

Jesus is King

A prayer of Mark Berryhill

The recently born goats are adorable, and joy is brought into our hearts as we see them for the first time.

The baby chicks can be held in the palm of ones hand, but seem at peace when near each other.

The guinea hens are quicker and more subtle than the snake, and make him lunch rather than being made lunch.

In the palm of the right hand of the Almighty God the universe is held.

Father, thank You for the beauty of Your creation, and most of all, thank You for Jesus!

In the name of the
Father, the Son and
the Holy Ghost

Amen and Amen
Copyright © 2008

Heart of a Child

A song of Mark Berryhill

Holy Ghost, may You cause love, joy, peace, longsuffering, gentleness, goodness, faith, meekness and temperance to reign in our hearts, and in the hearts of our children.

Holy Ghost, live and reign within the hearts of our children.

Holy Ghost, as the Shepherd gently leads His flock, lead the steps of the thoughts of the hearts of our children.

Holy Ghost, fall upon these precious lambs of Christ, even as on the day of Pentecost, and with Your skillful hands Almighty Father, as the potter with the clay, mold the hearts of our children.

In the name of the
Father, the Son and
the Holy Ghost

Amen and Amen
Copyright © 2008

The Beauty of Life

A prayer of Mark Berryhill

Did Mary fully understand how much she was loved by the Father to be chosen as the mother of His precious Son, Immanuel?

Did Mary fully understand the importance and power of the blood of her precious Son, Immanuel?

Did Mary fully understand that the world would be changed forevermore because of the unfathomable love of her precious Son, Immanuel?

Did Mary fully comprehend that "God with us" is the meaning and translation of her precious Son's name, Immanuel?

In the name of the
Father, the Son and
the Holy Ghost

Amen and Amen
Copyright © 2008

Light of the World

A prayer of Mark Berryhill

Holy Father, thank You for faithful mothers and dads who know that this is Your world.

Holy Father, thank You for the smiles of precious baby girls that bring forth such beauty and innocence into Your world.

Holy Father, thank You for the soft blue sky, white clouds floating as pillows, trees which seem to dance as Your wind gusts through them, for the dew covered grass, and for the variety of animals throughout Your world.

Holy Father, thank You for the majesty of Your sun as he rises and as he sets.

Holy Father, most of all, thank You for the birth of a precious baby boy who was born in the small town known as Bethlehem, and whose name is Jesus.

In the name of the
Father, the Son and
the Holy Ghost

Amen and Amen
Copyright © 2008

Jesus is Life

A prayer of Mark Berryhill

He came from Heaven to earth to do the will of His Father.

He came from Heaven to seek and save the lost which drift apart from His Father.

He came from Heaven to save the souls of His children, and to turn their eyes to His Father.

He came from Heaven to save you and me because the love within His heart for us is as the love that He possesses for His Father.

God is love!

In the name of the
Father, the Son and
the Holy Ghost

Amen and Amen
Copyright © 2008

Perfect Hearts

A song of Mark Berryhill

Have you considered the perfection with which the LORD created today?
Have you recently gazed at the beauty and brilliance of our LORD's shining stars as they dance and sing in His night sky?
Have you thanked our LORD today for your precious son, and for your precious daughter that He gave unto you because of His immense love for you?
Father, yesterday is a day already spent, while tomorrow is yet a dream and vision, teach us to live today by loving You with perfect hearts.

In the name of the
Father, the Son and
the Holy Ghost

Amen and Amen
Copyright © 2008

He will be Named Israel

A prayer of Mark Berryhill

Father, thank You for the beauty and love newborn children bring into our lives.

Father, may the hearts of our children be Your dwelling place.

Father, let the strength and greatness of America be Your unfathomable love for each child.

Father, with Your goodness and by Your enduring grace, the hearts of Your children will become hearts of gold, and hearts of silver.

Father, a tear of joy transforms into tears of love flowing as a racing river, and our hearts leap for joy as we pray, Immanuel, how great You are!

In the name of the
Father, the Son and
the Holy Ghost

Amen and Amen
Copyright © 2008

He is the Great I AM

A prayer of Mark Berryhill

Can you see the Father in His glory as He stands majestically over the very tallest of mountains, which He Himself designed?

Can you see the trees which reach into the Heavens and declare the glory of their Creator by singing songs of beauty unto Him?

Can you see the American Bald Eagle as he soars through the firmament of Heaven and begins his descent for his prey?

Can you see the bear's cubs in pursuit of their mother, as if it was their first time to ever see her?

Can you see the heart of pure love which resides within the Father, the Son, and the Holy Ghost?

In the name of the
Father, the Son and
the Holy Ghost

Amen and Amen
Copyright © 2008

The Love of JEHOVAH

A song of Mark Berryhill

JEHOVAH is love, and His hearts desire is for His children to trust Him.
JEHOVAH alone is His children's temporal and eternal provision and our lives are created to serve Him.
JEHOVAH dances and sings over His children with love in His heart, while His children dance and sing praises of joy unto Him.
JEHOVAH is great and no other can be compared unto Him.

In the name of the
Father, the Son and
the Holy Ghost

Amen and Amen
Copyright © 2008

Breath of Life

by Mark Berryhill

Dayspring

A Song of Mark Berryhill

She is very beautiful, and her heart is exceedingly tender.
Her smile radiates love, and JAH will prosper her with a journey of peace.
She is a beloved daughter of I AM THAT I AM, and His love for her truly is immeasurable!
Her pleasant manners bless all who meet her.
Her smile radiates love, and JEHOVAH has given her an exceedingly great faith.
She is an elegant woman, and her excellent habits have made her a beautiful person.
Her smile is so very captivating, and because of the diligent daily study of her Fathers Word, she is becoming a perfect woman.

In the name of the Father,
and of the Son,
and of the Holy Spirit.

Amen, and Amen.

A Word of Exhortation

A Song of Mark Berryhill

Love can only comprehend absolute victory, failure does not exist within the realm of true love.

Faith in God produces a life of tranquility and peace, while lack of faith in God promotes discontentment.

Hope can always be readily found when one's eyes are fixed steadfastly upon King Jesus.

Love surpasses all other qualities for within true love only perfection can be found.

Faith in God is brought to life through the diligent daily study of His Word.

Hope is a beautiful name of many precious little girls, and hope is even as they are, perfection absolute.

Love is more brilliant than the rays of the sun, for true love encourages, exalts, and exhorts.

In the name of the Father,
and of the Son,
and of the Holy Spirit.

Amen, and Amen.

Invaluable

A Song of Mark Berryhill

Love is as a fresh new morning, even as a painting of exquisite beauty, so is love.

Faith is brought to life by the diligent daily study of our Fathers Word.

Hope seeks only beauty and perfection, for she knows that there is no time for anything else.

Victory is translated as one who overcomes, and with perfect precision Christ overcame the world.

Salvation rests in the right hand of the Almighty, the shedding of Christ's blood has been fulfilled.

Peace is exceedingly greater than war, however, there is a time for both.

Prosperity even as wisdom issues forth protection, each of them truly are invaluable.

In the name of the Father,
and of the Son,
and of the Holy Spirit.

Amen, and Amen.

His Love for Her

A Song of Mark Berryhill

His love for her exceeds even the distance that it is from the farthest star of the west unto the farthest star of the east.

His love for her is even as great as the love God feels for His beloved Son Jesus.

His love for her gives her strength and courage, and has made her exceedingly beautiful.

His love for her cannot be written with mere words, for truly His love for her is immeasurable.

His love for her grows stronger with each passing day, His precious baby girl is becoming a mature woman of God.

His love for her will soon open her spiritual eyes, and cause her to realize the importance of the shedding of the blood of Gods perfect Lamb.

His love for her will soon cause her to fully appreciate the beauty of life.

In the name of the Father,
and of the Son,
and of the Holy Spirit.

Amen, and Amen.

Sovereign

A Song of Mark Berryhill

He provides you with the breath of life, should you not praise Him?

He provides you with the food that you eat, should you not thank Him?

He created you in His likeness because He loves you, should you not praise Him?

He created the heavens and the earth for you to enjoy, should you not thank Him?

He sent His Son to save you, should you not praise Him?

He is always faithful, and he is always true, should you not thank Him?

He is sovereign in its truest form, should you not love Him, and yet possess a reverent fear of Him?

In the name of the Father,
and of the Son,
and of the Holy Spirit.

Amen, and Amen.

The Beauty of Purity

A Song of Mark Berryhill

Her beauty is even as the beauty of a brilliant blooming flower, excellence in its purest form.

Her beauty is even as the beauty presented to the eyes by the exquisite smile of a precious young lady, excellence in its purest form.

Her beauty is even as the beauty of the youth of the youthful, excellence in its purest form.

Her beauty is even as the beauty found within the deepest and innermost faith, excellence in its purest form.

Her beauty is even as the beauty which is presented to the eyes by the artist's masterpiece revealing a beautiful woman lovingly cradling her twin baby girls, excellence in its purest form.

Her beauty is even as the beauty brought forth by a fresh new morning, excellence in its purest form.

Her beauty is even as the beauty of the unconditional love her Eternal Father possesses for her, excellence in its purest form.

In the name of the Father,
and of the Son,
and of the Holy Spirit.

Amen, and Amen.

Ancient of Days

A Song of Mark Berryhill

When you have found prosperity be thankful, and likewise during times of great distress be thankful.

As JAH causes the sun to rise and also to set, so likewise JAH carries you every moment of every day.

As the stars sing and dance before their Creator and bring joy into His heart, so likewise His heart craves your undivided attention.

As a faithful father works so diligently to provide for His family, so likewise God truly gives the provision.

As the beauty of a young mother gently cradling her newborn child, so likewise God watches over you and protects you.

As rest and relaxation are so vital for good health, so likewise is exercise.

Proper dieting helps to promote longevity, and He that is greater than all is the Ancient of Days.

In the name of the Father,
and of the Son,
and of the Holy Spirit.

Amen, and Amen.

His Masterpiece

A Song of Mark Berryhill

She is young and tender, and her beauty is so very captivating, truly she is a masterpiece of exquisite elegance.

Her beauty is even as a beautiful rose on its very best day, a masterpiece of exquisite elegance.

She is so very delicate and so exceedingly beautiful, she is a blessing to all who meet her, truly she is a masterpiece of exquisite elegance.

Her sweet disposition and excellent manners cause her to be very highly favored, truly she is a masterpiece of exquisite elegance.

Today she is a precious young lady, and yet but in a few tomorrows she will be a beautiful woman, a masterpiece of exquisite elegance.

In time she will become the great woman of faith her true Daddy created her to become, she truly is a masterpiece of exquisite elegance.

Her beauty exceeds what can be written with mere words, for truly she is a masterpiece of exquisite elegance.

In the name of the Father,
and of the Son,
and of the Holy Spirit.

Amen, and Amen.

Beloved Child

A Song of Mark Berryhill

Her beauty is even as the beauty of a brilliant blooming flower, an exquisite masterpiece of absolute perfection.

She is a shining star for her Heavenly Father, and His love for her is even as she is, an exquisite masterpiece of absolute perfection.

Her exquisite beauty can be likened to the beauty of a fresh new morning, a brilliantly painted painting of absolute perfection.

With the passing of time her faith will increase and will even be likened to the faith her Heavenly Father possesses, a faith of absolute perfection.

The love of her Heavenly Father will continually rest upon her, and will always be her guide, for it is a love of absolute perfection.

She is young and tender, and her beauty is so very captivating, she is even as a brilliantly painted painting of absolute perfection.

When she laughs her Daddy laughs with her, and when she cries her Daddy also cries, He created her to be a very special shining star, a star of absolute perfection.

In the name of the Father,
and of the Son,
and of the Holy Spirit.

Amen, and Amen.

An Eternal Love

A Song of Mark Berryhill

Love can only see the beauty of life, and love can only find perfection.

Faith in Jesus enables one to accomplish all things, for all things are possible to those who believe.

Hope is a beautiful name of many precious little girls, and hope even as the little ones are created perfect.

Love reaches from beyond the beginning and far beyond the end, for JEHOVAH was before the beginning, and will endure even beyond the end!

Faith in Jesus establishes strength in the weak, gives hope to the hopeless, and cause true life to be found.

Hope also brings forth life, light and love, for hope truly is even as love, perfection absolute.

Love blesses, and blesses and blesses some more, love merely produces more of what our Creator is, an Eternal love!

In the name of the Father,
and of the Son,
and of the Holy Spirit.

Amen, and Amen.

A Day of Thanksgiving

A Song of Mark Berryhill

Holy Father, thank You for this beautiful day.

Holy Father, thank You for sending Your Son and our Savior the Lord Jesus Christ to save us from our sins.

Holy Father, thank You for great grandparents.

Holy Father, thank You for our parents and for the love they extended to us during life.

Holy Father, thank you for our children and for the goodness that they bring into our lives.

Holy Father, teach us how to live while we are here on the earth.

Holy Father, thank You for our temporal lives, and most of all thank You for the eternal victory brought forth by the shedding of the blood of Your Beloved Son Jesus.

In the name of the Father,
and of the Son,
and of the Holy Spirit.

Amen, and Amen.

A Story of Grace

A Song of Mark Berryhill

Her beauty is even as the beauty of a fresh new morning during fall.

Her beauty is even as the beauty of a wife who is always truly faithful to her husband.

Her beauty is even as the beauty of the rays of the sun as they glisten on the great body of water.

Her beauty is even as the beauty of white sandy beaches which seemingly have no end.

Her beauty is even as the beauty of a beautiful mother who is always present when her children need her.

Her beauty is even as the beauty of untouched wildernesses of the far north, breathtaking, merely perfection absolute.

Her beauty is even as the beauty of the love her Heavenly Father has bestowed upon her, unconditional and without limit.

In the name of the Father,
and of the Son,
and of the Holy Spirit.

Amen, and Amen.

Because of Her

A Song of Mark Berryhill

Her beauty is as the beauty of a peaceful dew filled morning.

Her beauty is as the beauty of a brilliant rose of a magnificent garden of roses.

Her beauty is so very captivating, even as the beauty of a truly faithful wife, so is her beauty.

Truly it is the love and humility found within her heart that makes her so exceedingly special.

Her Heavenly Father painted her so perfectly because truly she is the innermost love of His heart.

Her beauty is so very captivating, even as the beauty of a gentle falling snow, so is her exquisite beauty.

In the name of the Father,
and of the Son,
and of the Holy Spirit.

Amen, and Amen.

By His Grace III

A Song of Mark Berryhill

His love for her can be neither weighed nor measured, truly it is immeasurable!
His love for her exceeds even the distance that it is from the farthest star of the
west unto the farthest star of the east.
His love for her is most accurately revealed in how beautifully He painted her.
His love for her is even as the scene of a young mother lovingly cradling her
newborn twin girls.
His love for her exceeds even the distance that it is to the deepest part of the
deepest ocean.
His love for her is even stronger today than on the day of her birth, truly she
has captured the heart of her Heavenly Father.
His love for her moved Him to send His precious Son to die for her, she lives
by His grace!

In the name of the Father,
and of the Son,
and of the Holy Spirit.

Amen, and Amen.

Eternal Life III

A Song of Mark Berryhill

Love is the greatest of all qualities, and in all reality only true love will always be found victorious.

Faith even as love is so very special, for it is by faith that the world will be overcome.

Hope walks hand in hand with faith, for it is by faith and hope that victory is issued forth.

Trust in God, He is your Creator, your Savior, your friend, and the true love found within your heart.

Peace is a blessing and gift from God, His truly beloved will ultimately walk and live therein unfortunately peace too often follows after war.

Life likewise is a blessing from God, He created everything beautiful, merely look at the perfection with which the universe functions.

Eternal Life is found only by faith in the atoning blood of Gods precious Son Jesus Christ, have you accepted Jesus as your Savior?

In the name of the Father,
and of the Son,
and of the Holy Spirit.

Amen, and Amen.

She is His Life

A Song of Mark Berryhill

His heart beats with her heart, when she cries He cries with her, and when she laughs He laughs with her.

She is the innermost love of His being, she is the very reason for His existence.

Her beauty exceeds even the beauty of the most beautiful, for the love found within her heart is a painting of explicit perfection.

Love and the quality thereof is greater than all, and her heart is even as the heart of her Heavenly Fathers, a love of exceeding beauty.

Even as love and hope walk hand in hand, so likewise she and her Heavenly Father walk hand in hand.

When J.A.H. created her, He merely created what He truly is, an Eternal Love.

Her beauty is even as the beauty of a brilliant, and so very delicate flower.

She is His life.

In the name of the Father,
and of the Son,
and of the Holy Spirit.

Amen, and Amen.

A Best Friend

A Song of Mark Berryhill

Love comprehends only victory, defeat cannot be found within the realm of true love.

Faith and hope walk hand in hand, while a prayer for peace is of exceeding great value.

Trust in God brings forth true contentment, only God is Creator, Savior, and Sustainer.

Your eternal salvation rests securely in the right hand of the Almighty, for the blood of His Son Jesus Christ is your life!

Joy is a gift from the Almighty, therefore live your life walking in His light.

Through the diligent study of God's Word, His people become as He is.

Jesus Christ is worthy, choose Him as your best friend.

In the name of the Father,
and of the Son,
and of the Holy Spirit.
Amen, and Amen.

By Faith

A Song of Mark Berryhill

Love is a gift from God, love is not merely for a moment or for a day; pure and true love is eternal.

Faith in the blood of Jesus Christ issues forth eternal salvation, have you truly placed your trust in Him?

Have you acknowledged Christ Jesus as your Lord and Savior, and been baptized with Him in baptism?

Hope likewise is a gift from our Eternal Father, can you imagine a world without hope?

Proper discipline promotes self-control, while lack thereof will ultimately bring forth destruction.

Intimacy between a husband and wife issues forth the greatest creation JEHOVAH has ever created, the newborn child!

True prosperity was purchased by the blood of Gods precious Son Jesus at His cross, His blood is eternal life!

In the name of the Father,
and of the Son,
and of the Holy Spirit.
Amen, and Amen.

An Incomprehensible Love

A Song of Mark Berryhill

JEHOVAH is greater than all, for it is by His infinite love and grace that we exist.

Jesus will never leave you or forsake you, He has already given everything for you.

Holy Spirit, thank you for Your relentless faithfulness.

Eternal Victory came into existence by the shedding of the blood of the Fathers innocent Lamb!

Faith is a beautiful name of many precious darling girls, and also it is by faith that the world will be overcome.

Hope likewise is a word of exceeding beauty, and it is by hope one can visualize the Son standing on the right hand of the Almighty.

The love of God is even as He is, an incomprehensible love.

In the name of the Father,
and of the Son,
and of the Holy Spirit.
Amen, and Amen.

A Song for Jesus

A Song of Mark Berryhill

Love is the most perfect and beautiful of all qualities, love is victory.

Eternal salvation is found only by your faith in the atoning blood of Gods precious Son Jesus Christ.

The diligent daily study of the Holy Bible helps to establish true faith.

Marriage and the sanctity thereof is a very special gift from a loving Father.

Beloved children also are a gift from God, for truly they are His workmanship.

When fulfilling the Great Commission of Jesus Christ is the desire of your heart, you find eternal victory!

Never underestimate the importance of rest and relaxation, God Himself rested after creating the Creation.

In the name of the Father,
and of the Son,
and of the Holy Spirit.
Amen, and Amen.

Heavenly Father

A Song of Mark Berryhill

Do you want to be more like your Heavenly Father, then study His Divinely inspired Holy Bible.

Are you truly submitted to the lead of the Holy Spirit as was Christ Jesus in the wilderness?

Is your heart truly concerned about the spiritual well-being of your neighbors as it should be?

Do you truly understand the importance of spreading the Holy Bible?

Are you using your time wisely, or are you allowing for it to be wasted?

Have you truly submitted your life and eternal salvation to Jesus Christ?

The blood of the lamb saved the Israelites in the days of Moses, and only the blood of the Lamb saves Gods people today!

In the name of the Father,
and of the Son,
and of the Holy Spirit.
Amen, and Amen.

JAH Reigns

A Song of Mark Berryhill

Love will always rule over the creation, as well as the created.
Obedience to your Heavenly Father will bring forth both temporal and eternal blessings, while disobedience would ultimately bring forth total destruction.
Eternal life is found by your faith in the atoning blood of Jesus Christ.
Grace is a gift from your Heavenly Father, you have His favor, His love for you is immeasurable.
Trust in God, He will always be there for you, His faithfulness truly is relentless.
Prayer likewise is a precious gift from the Father, never underestimate Gods attentiveness to the prayers of His saints.
Love will always rule over the creation, as well as the created, JAH is love!

In the name of the Father,
and of the Son,
and of the Holy Spirit.
Amen, and Amen.

A Journey of Faith

A Song of Mark Berryhill

She is young and tender and so exceedingly beautiful, her exquisite beauty is even as the beauty of a clear blue sky on a so very frigid January morning.

She is young and tender and so exceedingly beautiful, her exquisite beauty is even as the beauty of the leaves of trees changing color in Autumn.

She is young and tender and so exceedingly beautiful, her exquisite beauty is even as the beauty of an elegantly and meticulously decorated Christmas tree.

She is young and tender and so exceedingly beautiful, her exquisite beauty is even as the beauty of an artist's highly favored masterpiece, for truly she is her Heavenly Fathers Masterpiece.

She is young and tender and so exceedingly beautiful, her exquisite beauty is even as the beauty of the scene of her Heavenly Fathers angels continually watching over her.

She is young and tender and so exceedingly beautiful, her exquisite beauty is even as the beauty of a grandmothers faithful love for her beloved granddaughter.

She is young and tender and so exceedingly beautiful, her exquisite beauty is even as the beauty of a friendship that will endure throughout eternity.

In the name of the Father,
and of the Son,
and of the Holy Spirit.
Amen, and Amen.

A Perfect Heart

A Song of Mark Berryhill

She is so exceedingly beautiful, even as the beauty of the rays of the sun glistening on the great body of water as the sun begins his ascent, so is her exquisite beauty.

She is so exceedingly beautiful, even as the beauty of the picturesque scene of majestic snow-capped mountains of the far north, so is her exquisite beauty.

She is so exceedingly beautiful, even as the beauty of dancing stars in a brilliant night sky, so is her exquisite beauty.

She is so exceedingly beautiful, even as the picturesque scene of a gentle flowing stream, even a river of water of life, so is her exquisite beauty.

She is so exceedingly beautiful, even as the beauty of the artists painting which brings to life the brilliance of Gods pink and golden sun as he sets in the far west, so is her exquisite beauty.

She is so exceedingly beautiful, even as the beauty of a fresh new dew filled morning, so is her exquisite beauty.

She is so exceedingly beautiful, even as the beauty of the picturesque scene of a baby lamb enjoying the silence offered on the great ranch, so is her exquisite beauty.

In the name of the Father,
and of the Son,
and of the Holy Spirit.
Amen, and Amen.

The Purity of Love

A Song of Mark Berryhill

His love for her exceeds even the distance that it is from the farthest star of the west unto the farthest star of the east.

His love for her exceeds even the distance that it is from the farthest star of the north unto the farthest star of the south.

His love for her exceeds even the distance of the depth of the deepest of all oceans.

His love for her is immeasurable, for truly His love for her is so accurately revealed in how exquisitely beautiful He painted her.

His love for her will exceed time and the realm thereof, for truly His love for her is an incomprehensible love.

His love for her is even as the beauty of the artist's masterpiece that reveals a new mother gently cradling her newborn for the first time.

His love for her is even as the beauty of the scene of little ones with tightly clasped hands praying fervently to their Heavenly Father on Christmas day.

In the name of the Father,
and of the Son,
and of the Holy Spirit.
Amen, and Amen.

Immanuel

A Song of Mark Berryhill

Tomorrow is yet a dream and a vision while yesterday is a day already vanished, therefore live today to the fullest walking in the light of Jesus Christ.

Death follows life, and yet eternal life reigns over death by the blood of Gods Son Jesus Christ.

God loves to bless, and bless, and bless some more, take note of the beauty of the newborn children created by Jesus Christ.

The quality of faithfulness is truly more valuable than either gold or silver, and there is none as faithful as the Father of Jesus Christ.

Self-discipline promotes confidence and courage while lack of self-discipline promotes weakness, invest your time wisely in the Gospel of Jesus Christ.

Precious baby boys and darling little girls are an extension of their Creator, raise them in the daily admonition of their Lord Jesus Christ.

Eternal salvation is a gift of grace extended to you from a loving Father, eternal life is found only by your faith in the blood of Jesus Christ.

In the name of the Father,
and of the Son,
and of the Holy Spirit.

Amen, and Amen.

Immanuel III

A Song of Mark Berryhill

She will be called blessed by all generations.
She was obedient to the voice of Gods angel, and became a willing vessel for Her Heavenly Father.
She did not conceive her child JESUS by the seed of man, on the contrary, she conceived Immanuel by the Holy Spirit of her Heavenly Father.
She loved, she laughed and she cried.
She loved more, she laughed more, and she cried more.
In all the pain that JESUS experienced and suffered while on His cross, it was His mother that truly experienced the overwhelming heart of pain.
And yet suddenly she came to the realization of the importance of the shedding of the blood of Gods Lamb.
Seemingly infinite pain became infinite Victory!
Her name is Mary, and she alone was chosen as the mother of Immanuel.
She will be called blessed by all generations.

In the name of the Father,
and of the Son,
and of the Holy Spirit.
Amen, and Amen.

Word of Life

A Song of Mark Berryhill

Love was present before the creation came into existence, and love will reign beyond time, and the realm thereof.

JAH is love.

Faith and hope walk ever so closely, never ceasing to gently hold hands.

Peace is so very beautiful, even as a gentle falling rain revealed in an artist's masterpiece, so is the gift of peace and the tranquility brought forth thereby.

Grace is an undeserved gift lovingly extended to Gods children by the shedding of the blood of His Son Jesus Christ.

Marriage and the sanctity thereof is likewise a gift from the Almighty, precious little boys and darling little girls truly are an extension of their Creator.

In time of great prosperity love God, and likewise in time of great distress, rest in Him, and trust Him.

His mercy endures forever.

In the name of the Father,
and of the Son,
and of the Holy Spirit.
Amen, and Amen.

Because of God

A Song of Mark Berryhill

Precious little boys and darling little girls are merely an extension of their Creator, for truly He is the painter of brilliant masterpieces.

Faith knows the future and simply rests in the unrelenting love of the Almighty.

Hope is a beautiful name of many darling little girls, and it was likewise hope that helped to bring them into existence.

Godly persistence helps to bring forth victory, and always remember that everything in heaven and on earth belongs to JEHOVAH.

Kindness is even as a pleasant dew filled morning, fresh and so very comforting.

Gentleness in no way constitutes weakness, on the contrary she helps to breed peace, and peace issues forth tranquility.

Temperance and the practice thereof is an art, help us to live our lives submitted to your excellent Holy Spirit, Father God.

In the name of the Father,
and of the Son,
and of the Holy Spirit.
Amen, and Amen.

A Story of Victory

A Song of Mark Berryhill

She is young and so exceedingly beautiful, and yet maturity is walking with her. Her eyes are fixed steadfastly upon her Heavenly Father, and He is so very attentive to her prayers.

The beauty within her heart has yet to be painted, and yet the Master is ever presently ready to create.

Her brother on the other hand is young and strong and very handsome.

The love God possesses for His lambs is greater than either the realm of space or that of time, His love for His children as well as for His Creation is incomprehensible.

The favor of God is a gift extended to His children for only one reason, each of you are the reason for His existence.

At conception the journey of life begins, and likewise at conception the mortal body begins a race towards death!

Although physical appearance is so very fleeting, the spiritual beauty of hearts knows no death, His grace and His blood are Victorious!

In the name of the Father,
and of the Son,
and of the Holy Spirit.
Amen, and Amen.

A Story of Mercy

A Song of Mark Berryhill

Have you thanked your Heavenly Father today for creating His universe so perfectly?

Have you thanked JEHOVAH today for the beauty of His delicate roses?

Have you thanked your Wonderful Counselor today for the many blessings that He has bestowed upon you?

Have you thanked Immanuel today for residing within the innermost part of your heart?

Have you thanked the Prince of Peace today for the infinite mercy that He has placed with you?

Have you thanked your Creator today for having created you so meticulously and perfectly?

Have you thanked Abba today for His unwavering faithfulness?

In the name of the Father,
and of the Son,
and of the Holy Spirit.
Amen, and Amen.

Because of Love

A Song of Mark Berryhill

Love diligently seeks and searches for the true spiritual beauty brought forth during life.

Love has always reigned, and love always will reign, the Great JEHOVAH is love, life, and light.

Because of love precious little boys, and darling little girls come into existence.

Because of love precious little boys grow up and become great men of faith, and because of love darling little girl's blossom into great women of faith.

The Creator of love has no comprehension of failure, He is able to only understand absolute victory!

Love continues to exhort and encourage even as the end expeditiously approaches!

Love and grace are even as one, for truly love and grace cannot be separated.

Because of love God sent Victory from heaven to His cross, accept Jesus Christ as your Lord and Savior, and walk with Him, He is Eternal life!

In the name of the Father,
and of the Son,
and of the Holy Spirit.
Amen, and Amen.

Absolute Perfection

A Song of Mark Berryhill

Are you truly seeking the LORD with all of your heart, soul, mind, and strength?

Is serving God with a pure and perfect heart the desire of you heart?

Have you ever truly submitted your will to His Divine guidance, and received the baptism of the Holy Spirit?

If today were to be the last day of your mortal life, are you saved?

God sent Jesus to die for your sins because He loves you with all of His being!

God designed marriage to be between a man and a woman from the very beginning in the garden of Eden.

Marriage continues to produce Gods greatest creation ever, the newborn child, and He will sing over them with love in His heart this very night.

In the name of the Father,
and of the Son,
and of the Holy Spirit.
Amen, and Amen.

In His Time

A Song of Mark Berryhill

Have you told your Heavenly Father that you love Him today?

Are you truly submitted to the lead of His wonderful Holy Spirit?

Is evangelizing the world with Him and for Him the innermost desire of your heart?

Our mortal lives can be likened to a vapor, a shadow or even a mist, and yet the spirit lives eternally.

Generations of people rest in their graves, were they saved or were they lost?

The Holy Bible is a form of our Heavenly Father, it is in your best interest to know it, as well as to obey it.

My precious friends, it is the motive of the heart that is weighed by the Almighty!

In the name of the Father,
and of the Son,
and of the Holy Spirit.
Amen, and Amen.

A Story about JAH

A Song of Mark Berryhill

JAH truly is love, life, and light, and upon the innermost part of His heart the names of His children are recorded with the ink of blood.

JAH created the universe with meticulous precision, and only JAH provides the breath of life for the human race.

JAH and His love effortlessly supersede time and the realm thereof, and only JAH is Authority Supreme!

JAH is even as His creation, exceedingly greater than the human mind can either fathom or comprehend.

JAH and His children are even as one, for the precious Lamb of God washed the adorable baby lambs with His blood.

JAH is so exceedingly attentive to the prayers of His little ones, for truly they are the reason for His existence, and His angels are ever presently watching over them.

JAH is restricted by neither space nor time, and know with absolute certainty, He is Creator, Savior, and Sustainer, and there is no other who can be likened unto our JAH!

In the name of the Father,
and of the Son,
and of the Holy Spirit.
Amen, and Amen.

A Pure Heart

A Song of Mark Berryhill

Her exquisite beauty can be likened even to the beauty brought forth by the picturesque scene of seemingly endless fields of blooming bluebonnets surrounding the majestic lake.

Her exquisite beauty can be likened to the beauty brought forth by the picturesque scene of seven precious ducklings excitedly learning to swim for the first time.

Her exquisite beauty can be likened to the beauty brought forth by the picturesque scene of gentle baby deer drinking cold water of the lake on a so very pleasant afternoon.

Her exquisite beauty can be likened even to the beauty brought forth by the picturesque scene of graceful swans discovering new coves of water on the great lake.

Her exquisite beauty can be likened even to the beauty brought forth by the picturesque scene of playful fish soaring through the air as they chase the sun.

Her exquisite beauty can be likened even to the beauty brought forth by the picturesque scene of brilliant leaves of majestic trees changing colors in early Autumn.

Her exquisite beauty can be likened even to the beauty brought forth by the picturesque scene of a beautiful young woman praying fervently to her Heavenly Father, while on her knees with hands clasped ever so tightly.

In the name of the Father,
and of the Son,
and of the Holy Spirit.
Amen, and Amen.

Heed the Warning

A Writing of Mark Berryhill

In the year 2000 A.D. the LORD God displayed a rare, and yet very pronounced open vision.

Directly over the city of Del Rio, Texas which is in Val Verde County of the United States of America, God effortlessly painted a single cloud in the sky.

The cloud was precisely formed even as the Greek alphabet letter that is known as Omega.

Repent of your wickedness, and change your way says the Almighty, or My wrath will consume you even in an instant.

With your words you honor Me, but the actions of many of you speak differently, says the Almighty!

I created you in My likeness and in My image, walk before Me in truth, and with uprightness of heart.

From the rising of the sun even until the night watches seek My face, and then I will be readily found by you, says the Almighty.

How much time will My children invest in the Holy Bible while in the public schools of America each day?

How much time will the children of this great land spend in the Holy Bible today?

Fathers, walk My children daily in the Holy Bible, and cause them to become even as I AM, says the LORD God.

In the name of the Father,
and of the Son,
and of the Holy Spirit.
Amen, and Amen.

Breath of Life

A Song of Mark Berryhill

As the beauty of a fresh new morning, even so is her exquisite beauty.

As the beauty of a precious baby girl in a pretty new dress, being lovingly cradled by her mother, even so is her exquisite beauty.

As the beauty of the faithfulness of her Heavenly Father, even so is her exquisite beauty.

As the beauty brought forth by a day of peace and excellent tranquility, even so is her exquisite beauty.

As the beauty of seemingly endless star filled summer nights, even so is her exquisite beauty.

As the beauty of faithful friends, and faithful parents, even so is her exquisite beauty.

As the beauty brought forth by the eternal promises of her Heavenly Father, even so is her exquisite beauty.

In the name of the Father,
and of the Son,
and of the Holy Spirit.
Amen, and Amen.

We Love You Father

A Song of Mark Berryhill

Love existed even before the birth of the Creation, and love will effortlessly reign beyond the concept of time and the realm thereof.

As the blood began to gently trickle down the face of JESUS from the crown of thorns placed upon His head, the universe experienced the birth of infinite grace!

True faith can only comprehend victory absolute, for true faith soars only in the eternal realm.

A reaction follows every action, while what you practice today is what you will become tomorrow.

Place your trust in the LORD your God, He will never leave you, He is the love that has always been, the love that is, and the love that always will be!

If you want for God to be more prevalent in your life, study diligently, pray always, and fast often.

Obedience to the lead of the Holy Spirit is an art that we as Gods children pray to master, we love You Father!

In the name of the Father,
and of the Son,
and of the Holy Spirit.
Amen, and Amen.

A Very Special Daughter

A Song of Mark Berryhill

She is even more beautiful than the most beautiful of brilliant star filled night skies.

The innermost desire of her heart is to truly love and care for the less fortunate.

She is exceedingly elegant and graceful and so very perfect.

Her beauty produces a radiant bright light in a world filled with darkness.

She will with the passing of time become a woman of excellent understanding, and her wisdom and knowledge will be manifested to the world.

The beauty of her smile is so very captivating, and so very special, even as she is.

She is young and tender and so exceedingly fair, may she always radiate light, and life, and love as she does today!

In the name of the Father,
and of the Son,
and of the Holy Spirit.
Amen, and Amen.

A Life of Obedience

By Mark Berryhill

A Life of Obedience

A song of Mark Berryhill

Obedience to God, by His children, causes His smile to reach from the farthest star of the west unto the farthest star of the east.

Obedience to God causes the hopeless to become people of faith that soar on the wings of His angels.

Obedience to God causes the weak to become strong, and makes the poor to become rich.

Obedience to God by His children causes His heart to leap with gladness, and His light to shine even brighter.

Obedience to our Father fills our lives with goodness.

In the name of the
Father, the Son and
the Holy Ghost

Amen and Amen
Copyright © 2008

A Faithful King

A song of Mark Berryhill

Jesus is standing on the right hand of God because He is faithful and He is true.

Jesus is ruler over Heaven and earth because He is faithful and He is true.

Jesus willingly gave His life for you because He is faithful and He is true.

Jesus, thank You for the gift of life, and for the victory that You won at Your cross.

In the name of the
Father, the Son and
the Holy Ghost

Amen and Amen
Copyright © 2008

Who is Love?

A song of Mark Berryhill

Who spread forth the Heavens by the power of His right hand?
Who spoke and created light?
Who loves you more than any other?
Who is singing and dancing in Heaven today because a precious child received
Him as their personal Savior?
Who is love?
God is love.

In the name of the
Father, the Son and
the Holy Ghost

Amen and Amen
Copyright © 2008

A New Song

A song of Mark Berryhill

The clouds cry out unto the Almighty for permission to send forth rain, while the trees sing a new song and dance; a new dance before their Creator.

The earth groans because of the great wickedness which takes place upon her, and yet the stars unite as one and rejoice because of the greatness of the King of glory.

The cold winter breeze is fresh and crisp upon ones face, and yet the warm heated room is the place of rest for this afternoon; it is the day of the Lord.

Father, thank You for sending Jesus to save Your children.

In the name of the
Father, the Son and
the Holy Ghost

Amen and Amen
Copyright © 2008

Moral Excellence

A prayer of Mark Berryhill

A beautiful wife is a gift from God, while children are the delight of His heart. Good health is to be greatly appreciated, for she also is a gift from the Almighty. A beautiful day is much preferred over a day of wickedness, and those who keep the commandments of God will never taste death.

Goodness is a fruit of the Spirit, and is translated as one who is morally excellent.

In the name of the
Father, the Son and
the Holy Ghost

Amen and Amen
Copyright © 2008

Gift of Life

A prayer of Mark Berryhill

A beautiful woman is as a beautiful rose, fair to look upon, and as delicate as a newborn baby.

A beautiful wife is faithful to her husband even when all others have deserted him.

A woman of understanding realizes the importance of fulfilling the Great Commission of Christ, while the spiritually destitute woman considers only herself.

A beautiful woman knows that God blesses obedience, and halts blessings for disobedience.

In the name of the
Father, the Son and
the Holy Ghost

Amen and Amen
Copyright © 2008

A Prayer of Thanksgiving

A prayer of Mark Berryhill

Father, thank You for Your Word, and for the victory of Your Son Jesus at His cross.

Father, thank You for the precious gift of life.

Father, thank You for our beautiful children.

Father, cause Your love to reside within our hearts, and let Your infinite mercy shine, even as Your brilliant sun.

Father, thank You for warm sunny days.

Father, thank You for days that are lived in the joy and comfort of the Holy Ghost.

In the name of the
Father, the Son and
the Holy Ghost

Amen and Amen
Copyright © 2008

God of Love

A song of Mark Berryhill

Obedience is more valued than sacrifice to God, while rebellion to the Word of the Lord will cause the nation to fall.

Consider the beauty of life, and the eternal security shed forth because of the blood of the Lamb of God!

The leafless trees begin to softly sing once again, for they will soon be clothed with new leaves.

As the first warm ray of sunlight touches the flowers they begin to dance, and in unison bless their Creator.

The precious child is filled with excitement and shouts a shout of joy as she rapidly descends the playground slide.

When the educators of this world tell you they have something more important to teach the children than the Word of God, remove those educators.

In the name of the
Father, the Son and
the Holy Ghost

Amen and Amen
Copyright © 2008

Love and Purity

A song of Mark Berryhill

You desire to be forgiven, and yet you refuse to forgive.

You desire to serve God every moment of every day, and yet you rebel if His way is not your way.

You are beautiful beyond description as you walk in the light and obedience, and a rebel while walking in disobedience.

You and I are called to a life of obedience to our God, not a life of rebellion.

You have a heart of gold, because love and purity is the desire of your heart.

In the name of the
Father, the Son and
the Holy Ghost

Amen and Amen
Copyright © 2008

The Beauty of Love

A song of Mark Berryhill

Life is precious and she is eternal.

Love is the most beautiful of all qualities, and love will never fail you.

Hope is brought forth to the hopeless by the blood of Jesus Christ, and He is the Son of God.

Faith in Jesus is how we will overcome the world, and by His lead we will be victorious.

The birth of a newborn child is a gift from God, and is confirmation of His love for you.

In the name of the
Father, the Son and
the Holy Ghost

Amen and Amen
Copyright © 2008

A Story of Grace

A prayer of Mark Berryhill

The act of self-discipline brings forth great rewards, while the lack thereof would eventually steal the very joy of living.

Life is good and to be enjoyed, and always remember we are here for but one reason, to serve our Creator.

Light came into existence by the Word of God, and our lives are to be lived in the light of His Son Jesus.

Thank You Father, for parents who raise their children in the daily admonition and nurture of You.

Jesus is love, and it is by His grace and His grace alone whereby we are saved.

In the name of the
Father, the Son and
the Holy Ghost

Amen and Amen
Copyright © 2008

In His Arms

A song of Mark Berryhill

In His arms the lamb is gently carried, and your name is written upon His heart.

In His arms the world is held, and by His wisdom we exist.

In His arms the child that He created is held, and His love for the child will exist throughout eternity.

In His arms the breath of life is held, and in His blood our eternal life is found.

In His arms the stars unite as one and glorify Him with song, and within His arms

His creation is held.

In the name of the
Father, the Son and
the Holy Ghost

Amen and Amen
Copyright © 2008

In the Light of Christ

A prayer of Mark Berryhill

Living for Christ brings forth great joy into our hearts, and He and He alone is the Savior.

Life is to be savored and yet lived for others, not oneself.

Live your life to the fullest in the light of Jesus Christ, and let His love in you shine forth throughout the world.

The precious child held in your arms this very day is confirmation from God of His immense love for you.

Life on earth is as a horse race, exciting and finished very quickly.

In the name of the
Father, the Son and
the Holy Ghost

Amen and Amen
Copyright © 2008

The Sovereignty of JEHOVAH

A song of Mark Berryhill

JEHOVAH raised His Son Jesus Christ from the grave and set Him on His right hand because He was obedient even unto death.

JEHOVAH rules over Heaven and earth and Jesus Christ is His Son.

JEHOVAH spoke and created light and with His delicate hands He created the earth and the beauty she possesses.

JEHOVAH is light and in Him no darkness can be found.

JEHOVAH sent forth His Son to die for you because He loves you even as He loves His beloved Son.

In the name of the
Father, the Son and
the Holy Ghost

Amen and Amen
Copyright © 2008

Love of a Mother

A song of Mark Berryhill

Mere words can not describe the unfathomable brilliance of JEHOVAH!
Mere words can neither describe nor calculate the amount of love within the heart of JEHOVAH!
Mere words can neither describe nor express the joy caused within the heart of a mother as she delivers her first born son, which was created by the delicate hands of
JEHOVAH!
Mere words are unable to tell of the greatness of JEHOVAH!

In the name of the
Father, the Son and
the Holy Ghost

Amen and Amen
Copyright © 2008

A Bright Light

A song of Mark Berryhill

Jesus Christ is from everlasting to everlasting, and in His blood a fountain of youth is found.

Immanuel is the same yesterday, today and for all of tomorrows; and His faithfulness to His children will endure throughout infinity.

The Lamb of God is the bright light in a world filled with darkness, and with Him as your friend hope and joy are found.

Lion of Judah, we love You with every fiber of our existence, thank You for Your life of obedience Lord Jesus Christ.

In the name of the
Father, the Son and
the Holy Ghost

Amen and Amen
Copyright © 2008

I AM

A prayer of Mark Berryhill

Why do you seek after the things of the world when it is I AM that you need?
Why does the sun rise and set except it be that I AM has established it so?
Why do the stars of Heaven unite as one and sing praises to I AM except He,
ordain it to be so?
Why does a mother love her children more than she loves herself except I AM
reside in her heart?
Why does God love you with all that He is, because He is I AM THAT I AM!

In the name of the
Father, the Son and
the Holy Ghost

Amen and Amen
Copyright © 2008

A Song and a Dance

A prayer of Mark Berryhill

Will you lay down your life for Jesus if He calls you to do so?

Will you obey His voice even though others desire to lead you down the path of destruction?

Will you sing and dance with all of your might before the King of glory this very day as He calls you to do so?

Will you marry the mate He has chosen for you, or will you be lead astray by the ignorance of others?

Will you love God with every fiber of your being this very day, or will you be lead astray by the wicked?

In the name of the
Father, the Son and
the Holy Ghost

Amen and Amen
Copyright © 2008

Creator of Life

A prayer of Mark Berryhill

JEHOVAH has sent rain and the young pecan tree that seemed near death is now brilliantly clothed with beautiful shiny new leaves.

The baby live oak trees struggled during the cold winter but now rejoice about their new leaves, and because warm rays of sun have searched them out and found them.

The butterfly is painted a brilliant yellow and patiently flutters northward, even as the breath of God moves toward the south.

The small withered cactus has surprisingly produced violet flowers of elegance, and we get to be thankful to see yet another magnificent creation, created by the Creator of life.

In the name of the
Father, the Son and
the Holy Ghost

Amen and Amen
Copyright © 2008

My Beloved America

A song of Mark Berryhill

America, my beloved America, put away the things of this world and place your eyes upon Jesus.

America, my beloved America, why have you allowed your heart to become ensnared in the works of the enemy?

America, my beloved America, as the young boy hugs his precious baby sister as a confirming sign of His love for her, so was the resurrection of the Son of God by the Father a sign of the Fathers unfathomable love for you!

The American Bald eagle soars on the wings of the angels of the Everlasting Father, my beloved America.

In the name of the
Father, the Son and
the Holy Ghost

Amen and Amen
Copyright © 2008

In Pursuit of God

A song of by Mark Berryhill

Victory follows after unity, while defeat is acknowledged soon after dissension.
Victory for both you and I came to fruition at the cross of Jesus Christ.
Victory and victorious are two words that must be placed at the forefront of
the hearts of our children.
Victory never settles for defeat, while the defeated are only those who do not
believe God raised His Son Jesus Christ from the grave.
Victory and the ultimate manifestation of her far outweigh the temporary
struggles and obstacles presented in the pursuit of her.

In the name of the
Father, the Son and
the Holy Ghost

Amen and Amen
Copyright © 2008

A Lamb without Blemish

A prayer of Mark Berryhill

Jesus completed His work for the Father faithfully and is therefore set on the right hand of the Almighty.

Jesus was born of a virgin named Mary, while His earthly father was named Joseph.

Jesus Christ is the same yesterday, today and forever, and no other was found as a Lamb without blemish.

Jesus loves you more than any other and He will never forsake you; He is faithful and true.

Jesus is the light of the world and in His blood your salvation securely rests.

In the name of the
Father, the Son and
the Holy Ghost

Amen and Amen
Copyright © 2008

Greatly Beloved

A song of Mark Berryhill

Love and truth are dancing with each other, while unity and peace are singing a song about grace.

Love comes to life as a mother cradles her newborn son for the first time; while a father realizes love as he cradled his precious newborn daughter for the first time.

Love is the very being of God, and besides Him there is no other!

Love is what a newly wed couple experience as they are together for the first time.

Love, in its purest form, was most accurately demonstrated by the Son of God as

He hung on the cross for the sins of His greatly beloved.

In the name of the
Father, the Son and
the Holy Ghost

Amen and Amen
Copyright © 2008

Rain of God

A song of Mark Berryhill

While the flowers are singing a new song, the trees are dancing because of the falling rain of God.

The shrubs and cactus shout as joy fills their hearts because of the falling rain of God.

Love, life and laughter are renewed once again because of the falling rain of God.

Remember wise friends, food is abundantly produced because of the falling rain of God.

Consider carefully the importance of these words dearly beloved, the study of the

Word of God, by the children, produces the falling rain of God.

In the name of the
Father, the Son and
the Holy Ghost

Amen and Amen
Copyright © 2008

150

A Story of Faith

A prayer of Mark Berryhill

Love and joy hold hands as they walk beside one another, and peace pursues the longsuffering.

Gentleness and goodness are as one for good is always gentle.

Placing your faith in Jesus Christ for your eternal salvation is the most important decision of your life.

Meekness is not a sign of weakness; on the contrary it is confirmation of discipline.

Temperance is translated as self-control and she helps to produce a life full of love.

In the name of the
Father, the Son and
the Holy Ghost

Amen and Amen
Copyright © 2008

The Love of Immanuel

A prayer of Mark Berryhill

Immanuel is dancing in Heaven this very day because of His immense love for you!

Immanuel is singing songs of beauty in Heaven this very day because of His immense love for you!

Immanuel is weeping tears of joy this very day because of His immense love for you!

Immanuel is faithful and true and He will never leave you nor forsake you because of His immense love for you!

In the name of the
Father, the Son and
the Holy Ghost

Amen and Amen
Copyright © 2008

A Dedication to the American Cowgirl

A song of Mark Berryhill

The cowboy quickly realizes the overwhelming power that God has bestowed upon the bull as the gate is opened, and a few seconds become what seems as an eternity to the rigid cowboy.

The cowgirl races against the clock as she gracefully leads her horse around each barrel and then darts back toward the finish line.

The young cowboy is wearing a helmet for protection as the gate opens and gives all that he has to ride the contrary lamb.

The American flag is proudly held and exalted by a cowgirl that is more beautiful than the most beautiful of roses, and yet she as a rose is elegant and so very fragile.

In the name of the
Father, the Son and
the Holy Ghost

Amen and Amen
Copyright © 2008

Thank You Father

A song of Mark Berryhill

Father, thank You for sending Your Son Jesus to die for our sins because of Your immense love for us.
Thank You for the gift of Your Word.
Thank You for the gift of the Holy Ghost.
Thank You for the gift of our precious children, the born and soon to be born.

In the name of the
Father, the Son and
the Holy Ghost

Amen and Amen
Copyright © 2008

JEHOVAH Reigns

A prayer of Mark Berryhill

Within the right hand of JEHOVAH, the universe is held.

The birth of a beloved child is a gift extended from the right hand of JEHOVAH.

Love will endure throughout infinity, and He securely rests sitting upon the right hand of JEHOVAH.

Your next breath of life is a precious gift extended by the right hand of JEHOVAH.

JEHOVAH reigns over Heaven and earth, and by the power of His right hand He spread forth the Heavens.

In the name of the
Father, the Son and
the Holy Ghost

Amen and Amen
Copyright © 2008

Within the Heart of Jesus

A song of Mark Berryhill

The beauty brought forth by the flowers reveals the beauty that resides within the heart of Jesus.
The beautiful smile of a precious baby reveals the beauty that resides within the heart of Jesus.
Brilliant dancing stars in the night sky reveal the beauty that resides within the heart of Jesus.
The love of a faithful wife likewise reveals the love that resides within the heart of Jesus.

In the name of the
Father, the Son and
the Holy Ghost

Amen and Amen
Copyright © 2008

Child of Christ

A song of Mark Berryhill

Life began in a garden, and the caring for her produces good health.

Life is good and for we who keep the commandments of Christ, we will never taste death.

Life is brought forth because a man and a woman love each other, and the couple is greatly beloved of the Lord.

Life is exciting, and the journey she brings forth is up to you a child of Christ.

In the name of the
Father, the Son and
the Holy Ghost

Amen and Amen
copyright © 2008

Blessed of JAH

A song of Mark Berryhill

Blessed is the man to whom God has given many children.
Blessed is the woman to whom God has given many children.
Blessed is the man to whom God has given good health, thereby enabling him to work.
Blessed is the woman to whom God has given good health, thereby enabling her to care for the children.
Blessed is the nation that walks daily with JAH.

In the name of the
Father, the Son and
the Holy Ghost

Amen and Amen
Copyright © 2008

Love of God

A prayer of Mark Berryhill

Thank You for making Your children so very unique, Almighty Father.
Thank You for the free gift of Your Son Jesus, and for our precious children,
Almighty Father.
Thank You for the beauty of today, Almighty Father.
Thank You for Your faithfulness to Your people, Almighty Father.

In the name of the
Father, the Son and
the Holy Ghost

Amen and Amen
Copyright © 2008

What is His Name?

A song of Mark Berryhill

God is doing cartwheels in Heaven because another precious baby girl has been born into the world.

God is singing a song of beauty because another precious baby boy has been delivered into the world.

The baby girl looks almost exactly as does her mother, how great is the God of Israel?

The baby boy is an exact replica of his daddy, how great is the God of Israel?

Tell me His name and the name of His Son if you can dearly beloved.

In the name of the
Father, the Son and
the Holy Ghost

Amen and Amen
Copyright © 2008

Lamb of God

A song of Mark Berryhill

Although rain causes iron to stain varnished wood, no stain can be found against you because of the power of the blood of the Lamb of God.

Although the sight of two precious daughters clothed in identical dresses brings forth gladness into the heart of their mother, true joy for the mother is brought forth because of the girl's eternal salvation which was bought and paid for by the blood of the Lamb of God.

Although beautiful dancing rainbows are a great sight, victory for you and I is found in the eternal power of the blood of the Lamb of God.

Although rain is good for growing food, and drinking water is good for health, the fountain of youth is found in the precious blood of the Lamb of God.

In the name of the
Father, the Son and
the Holy Ghost

Amen and Amen
Copyright © 2008

A Soft Falling Rain

A prayer of Mark Berryhill

Listen carefully and you will hear the trees singing songs of praises to their Creator because of the abundance of rain.

Flowers are holding hands and likewise rejoice because of the abundance of their Creator's rain.

The grass is dancing and so very thankful for the abundance of their Creator's rain.

God has once again proven His faithfulness to His children and to His earth by sending forth an abundance of His rain.

In the name of the
Father, the Son and
the Holy Ghost

Amen and Amen
Copyright © 2008

The Love of JAH

A prayer of Mark Berryhill

Love transcends all other qualities, while our faith in Jesus Christ is how we will overcome the world.

Love supersedes all other gifts, and hope is a light brought forth to people dwelling in darkness.

Love surpasses the highest and farthest star of the Heavens, while your faith in the blood of Jesus Christ is where eternal life is found.

Love is dancing with hope, while faith sings a song with words of great beauty.

JAH is love and by the power of His right hand, the breath of life is held.

In the name of the
Father, the Son and
the Holy Ghost

Amen and Amen
Copyright © 2008

A Time of Victory

A song of Mark Berryhill

Will you obey the Lord even when His will does not coincide with your own?
Will you truly submit your life to the lead of the Holy Spirit as you vowed in your time of need?
Will you exalt Jesus in the difficult times as well as in the times of great triumph?
Will you give Him precious children that He longs for, or will you close your ears to His call and harden your heart against His voice?
Will you ever learn to enjoy the beauty of life as you walk hand in hand with your Almighty Father?

In the name of the
Father, the Son and
the Holy Ghost

Amen and Amen
Copyright © 2008

Sound of a Trumpet

A prayer of Mark Berryhill

The end is at hand, and yet many people have hearts seemingly made of stone.
The end is at hand, and yet many people throughout the world have not come
to know the Gospel of Jesus Christ.
The end is at hand, and yet many educators are filled with the spirit of ignorance,
and have not any knowledge of the Holy Scriptures.
The end is at hand; will you be saved as your trumpet sounds?

In the name of the
Father, the Son and
the Holy Ghost

Amen and Amen
Copyright © 2008

A Dance with God

A prayer of Mark Berryhill

When Jesus calls you to preach His Word, will you obey Him or pretend as if you did not hear His voice?

When Jesus calls you to a life of obedience, will you truly pursue a life of obedience or pretend that you did not hear the whisper of His voice in your heart?

When Jesus calls you to deny yourself and take up your cross daily, will you heed His advice or ignore Him as they in the day of provocation?

When will you truly give your heart to your Savior?

In the name of the
Father, the Son and
the Holy Ghost

Amen and Amen
Copyright © 2008

Day of Salvation

By Mark Berryhill

A Life of Beauty

A song of Mark Berryhill

The sons of thunder spoke this morning, and Jehovah sent a much needed rain.
Precious puppies hardly able to walk one week can seemingly run with the wind the next week.
Life is to be lived to the fullest, walking in the light of Jesus Christ.
God blesses nations and people that seek Him through His Word daily; and destroys those who refuse.
Can you hear the beauty of the song Jehovah is singing over you this very day?

In the name of the
Father, the Son and
the Holy Ghost

Amen and Amen
Copyright © 2008

By Design of the Father

A prayer of Mark Berryhill

Self-discipline, when properly directed, produces astounding results.
True love never abandons and looks only for good while abhorring evil.
Life is as a day quickly spent; therefore seek the face of the King.
The creation that was created by Jehovah and belongs to Him is as He is, greater than what mere human words can state.

In the name of the
Father, the Son and
the Holy Ghost

Amen and Amen
Copyright © 2008

Victory

A song of Mark Berryhill

Cleave unto Jesus for He is your strength and your salvation.
Sing unto the Lord a new song, and dance before Him with all of your might.
Pursue love and turn from hate.
Grace is a gift from the Most High, are you walking therein?
In Christ Jesus defeat can never be found, only victory!

In the name of the
Father, the Son and
the Holy Ghost

Amen and Amen
Copyright © 2008

Without Measure

A song of Mark Berryhill

In the times of great difficulty, we will seek Your face King Jesus, and in the times of great abundance, we will seek Your face King Jesus.
With You ever presently before our faces and by our sides, life is a blessing.
Anoint us with Your Holy Spirit Almighty Father and walk us in the light of Your Son Jesus.
Teach us Your will and Your way Everlasting Father.

In the name of the
Father, the Son and
the Holy Ghost

Amen and Amen
Copyright © 2008

Art of JEHOVAH

A song of Mark Berryhill

The sun rises and then she sets even at the command of the Great JEHOVAH. His clouds are gathered together and then He commands them to pour rain upon an obedient people; for He is the Great JEHOVAH.

The American Bald Eagle soars through the firmament of Heaven even by the Divine Will of JEHOVAH.

Precious little boys and darling little girls issue forth from the bodies of their mothers by the genius of the Great JEHOVAH.

He is attentive to the prayers of His saints, and nothing or nobody can stop the Divine Will of the Great JEHOVAH!

In the name of the
Father, the Son and
the Holy Ghost

Amen and Amen
Copyright © 2008

A Day with God

A song of Mark Berryhill

The cool water of the beautiful lake is refreshing and brings joy into the heart of this young man.

A strong wind causes fierce white caps upon the open lake and makes one realize the over-whelming strength of JEHOVAH.

Rain has recently fallen and the lake is full, even to the brim, and the variety of the colors of the trees demonstrates the brilliance of the artwork of God.

Fishermen wait patiently for the next strike and savor every moment of the beauty of JEHOVAH's creation.

Life is exceedingly good when the eyes of man are focused upon the Creator not the created.

In the name of the
Father, the Son and
the Holy Ghost

Amen and Amen
Copyright © 2008

A Prayer of Verity

A prayer and a song of Mark Berryhill

Praise JEHOVAH in His sanctuary; yes praise Him from the rising of the sun until the setting of the sun.

Exalt JEHOVAH sons and daughters of the Most High; let His glory overshadow each one of you.

Glorify the Great JEHOVAH with song, with verity, and with the sacrifice of thanksgiving.

Bless JEHOVAH the Father of all with prayers of thankfulness.

In the name of the
Father, the Son and
the Holy Ghost

Amen and Amen
Copyright © 2008

Can You See?

A prayer of Mark Berryhill

With JEHOVAH in the daily lives of the children, prosperity will flow as a racing river.

Can you keep your physical body alive without the Spirit of the Almighty?

Love is from everlasting to everlasting and the Creator of love is the Everlasting Father.

It is by faith that the Christians will overcome the world, for it is Jesus Christ that has been given all authority over Heaven and earth by the Father.

The perfect twinkle in the eyes of His children and the twinkling of the stars at night must be the reason for His existence.

In the name of the
Father, the Son and
the Holy Ghost

Amen and Amen
Copyright © 2008

A Time of Gratitude

A prayer of Mark Berryhill

Faithful friends are a blessing from God; can you be considered a true friend?
Holy Spirit, cause truth to reign within our hearts, and within our lives.
JEHOVAH, thank You for the beauty and brilliance of Your magnificent creation.
Immanuel let Your love and infinite mercy flow down from Your throne of grace.
Blessed be the Great JEHOVAH, who is the Beginning and the End.

In the name of the
Father, the Son and
the Holy Ghost

Amen and Amen
Copyright © 2008

A Pure Heart

A prayer of Mark Berryhill

Why does the water of one lake appear blue while the water of a different lake appears to be as red as blood?

Is blood blue while in the body, and yet red when outside of the body of oneself?

The grass is tall and green and the cattle seem content with the amount of food JEHOVAH has prepared for them.

The long neck of the stork, and the long legs of the stork bring immediate attention to her; I wonder if she will soon be called to carry a newborn baby to the mother thereof?

The power and speed of the new boats motor is exhilarating, and lives are to be lived spreading the Gospel of Jesus Christ with understanding and enthusiasm.

In the name of the
Father, the Son and
the Holy Ghost

Amen and Amen
Copyright © 2008

Rain of JEHOVAH

A prayer of Mark Berryhill

The blooming flowers of the sage range in color from a soft light violet to a brilliant dark violet because of the recent rain sent by JEHOVAH.

Delicate birds are singing a new song this morning as they wade in the recent rain sent by JEHOVAH.

The grass, which seemed near death, is now a beautiful sparkling green because of the recent rain sent by JEHOVAH.

The air is fresh and clean because of the recent rain sent by JEHOVAH.

Young kings and darling princesses are clothed majestically as they leave the House of JEHOVAH this morning; the Holy One who sent the recent rain.

In the name of the
Father, the Son and
the Holy Ghost

Amen and Amen
Copyright © 2008

Breath of Life

A song of Mark Berryhill

How many days will your mortal body exist on the earth; would it not be wise to serve the Great JEHOVAH?

Will your heart continue to beat when your heart is told to beat no more by the Great JEHOVAH?

Do you not long to see the paradise prepared for you by the Great JEHOVAH?

Oh that the people of this beautiful land would seek the face of the Great JEHOVAH!

In the name of the
Father, the Son and
the Holy Ghost

Amen and Amen
Copyright © 2008

Immanuel

A prayer of Mark Berryhill

The greatest gift ever given to the human race came in the form of a little boy born to a virgin named Mary.

His Father loves you so much that He allowed for Immanuel, His precious Son, to be spit upon, ridiculed, mocked and ultimately hung from a cross.

Why did God choose this particular child who will become known throughout the world as the Savior; it is by His blood and only by His blood that we are redeemed back to the Father.

If you are sad, you should not be, you should be rejoicing in the victory of Gods child Immanuel.

In the name of the
Father, the Son and
the Holy Ghost

Amen and Amen
Copyright © 2008

The Love of I AM

A song of Mark Berryhill

You called unto Me in your time of trouble and I delivered you; why do you resist in keeping the vows you vowed to Me, My precious son?

You called unto Me in your time of great despair and I delivered you; why do you walk contrary to the vows you covenanted with Me, My precious daughter?

You are the apple of My eye My precious son, My heart delights in teaching You My ways!

You are the inner most love in My heart My precious daughter; it is My immense love for you that carries Me through the days!

My son and My precious daughter, My love for each of you will endure throughout the realm of time.

In the name of the
Father, the Son and
the Holy Ghost

Amen and Amen
Copyright © 2008

Brilliance of Immanuel

A song of Mark Berryhill

As a beautiful rose races forth for the soft falling rain, so you will seek My face children of Israel.

As wind causes the white capping of waves on a large body of water, My Spirit will saturate your heart with My Word, children of Israel.

As soft music of the brilliant musician is pleasant to the ear, so are your prayers pleasant to Me, My precious children of Israel.

As the majestic oak tree reaches toward the Heavens and as the arms of a precious child grasp for the comfort of the hug of the mother, so will you long for the comfort of My Holy Spirit, My precious children of Israel.

In the name of the
Father, the Son and
the Holy Ghost

Amen and Amen
Copyright © 2008

Immanuel Overcame

A song of Mark Berryhill

Although love is the greatest of all gifts, it is by faith that the world will be overcome.

Love produces life and beauty, while hate attempts to steal the very reason of the creation.

A child is a blessing and gift from JEHOVAH, and the child is safely placed within the innermost place of His heart.

At the cross of Jesus the victory was won, for it is by His innocent blood eternal life is found.

You will give an account of your actions to the King of kings, and the Lord of Lords; are you prepared for the consequences of those actions?

In the name of the
Father, the Son and
the Holy Ghost

Amen and Amen
Copyright © 2008

By the Strength of JEHOVAH

A song of Mark Berryhill

The sky is clear and one can almost see JEHOVAH sitting on His throne.
The trees reach into the Heavens and the hand of JEHOVAH can almost be
reached if one was resting at the top of the majestic tree.
Although the small seed appears insignificant to the natural eye, it is this very
seed that becomes the tree almost enabling one to talk with JEHOVAH eye
to eye, and heart to heart.
JEHOVAH is pleading for an obedient people, and He sent His precious Son
Jesus to prove His immense love for you; walk your spirit in the light of His
truth, my precious child.

In the name of the
Father, the Son and
the Holy Ghost

Amen and Amen
Copyright © 2008

Brilliance of JEHOVAH

A prayer of Mark Berryhill

As the beauty of elegant blooming flowers of the sage, so is the beauty of a faithful bride adorned for her husband by the Great JEHOVAH.

As the rose in a fertile garden rejoices over the soft falling rain of JEHOVAH, so likewise rejoices a beautiful young wife over the conception of her soon to be child.

The most brilliant artist there has ever been or ever will be is the Great JEHOVAH.

So as the heart of the mother leaps for joy at the completion of the delivery of her precious child, so likewise the heart of the Great JEHOVAH leaps for joy at the faithfulness of your prayers.

So as the beauty of the sunrise, and as the beauty of the sunset, so is the beauty of the love JEHOVAH has bestowed upon you.

In the name of the
Father, the Son and
the Holy Ghost

Amen and Amen
Copyright © 2008

Word of JEHOVAH

A prayer of Mark Berryhill

JEHOVAH sent Elijah to Bethel and he obeyed, will you likewise obey the Word of JEHOVAH?

JEHOVAH sent Elijah to Jericho and he obeyed, will you likewise obey the Word of JEHOVAH?

JEHOVAH sent Elijah to Jordan and he obeyed, will you likewise obey the Word of JEHOVAH?

JEHOVAH called out to the governors of the land, but will they likewise obey the Word of JEHOVAH?

In the name of the
Father, the Son and
the Holy Ghost

Amen and Amen
Copyright © 2008

Son of Man

A song of Mark Berryhill

As a mother loves her precious daughter, and as a father loves his son, so is My love for all of My children, says the Great I AM!

As the bald cypress tree near the river began as an insignificant seed, and now reaches into the Heavens, so likewise I will cause wisdom to flourish in your hearts, says the Great JEHOVAH!

How is it possible for a turtle to live above the water and below the water, and yet man cannot, asks the Great King?

Can you tell Me the number of the colors of My brilliant flowers, Son of man?

In the name of the
Father, the Son and
the Holy Ghost

Amen and Amen
Copyright © 2008

Light of the World

A prayer of Mark Berryhill

Jesus Christ is the same yesterday, today and forever.
Jesus Christ would have you listen and consider before speaking.
Jesus Christ offered His life for you because of His great love for you.
Jesus Christ has been given all authority over Heaven and earth by the Father;
submit your spirit to His Word, the light of the world.

In the name of the
Father, the Son and
the Holy Ghost

Amen and Amen
Copyright © 2008

Above His Thunder

A song of Mark Berryhill

Love transcends all other qualities, and she pursues only that which is good.
Faith is a gift from God, and by faith the world will be overcome.
Hope walks beside love, and will live eternally.
Trust is best placed in Jesus Christ; He is faithful in the time of great distress,
and also in the time of great prosperity.

In the name of the
Father, the Son and
the Holy Ghost

Amen and Amen
Copyright © 2008

Will you obey?

A song of Mark Berryhill

Have you given your heart to Jesus Christ?
Today, will you trust Him with your eternal destiny?
Have you acknowledged Him as your Lord and Savior, the Ruler of your life?
He is calling you today, listen to His voice, and surrender your spirit to Him!
What is a day or one hundred and twenty years when compared to eternity?

In the name of the
Father, the Son and
the Holy Ghost

Amen and Amen
Copyright © 2008

I AM THAT I AM

A song of Mark Berryhill

As an acorn falls from a live oak tree and perishes because it is not planted, so has
America the beautiful squandered the great wealth thereof.
The people of the United States of America seem to have time for everything except for time to serve God; she is therefore on the edge of spiritual and financial destitution.
The few with great wealth have horded their wealth while the flock of God has been starved for His Word, and for His love.
Therefore sons and daughters of wealth, because you have neglected My precious lambs and not set it in your hearts to feed them, prepare to meet your Maker, I AM THAT I AM!

In the name of the
Father, the Son and
the Holy Ghost

Amen and Amen
Copyright © 2008

A Prayer of Truth

A prayer of Mark Berryhill

Thank You Father for the beauty of Your creation.

Thank You Father for Your Word that gives Your people an insight into Your heart.

Thank You Father for precious sons and darling daughters that are so special in our eyes.

Thank You Father for being greater than all, for by Your Divine power life is sustained.

Thank You Father for the blood of Your Son Jesus Christ, the King of kings and Lord of lords.

In the name of the
Father, the Son and
the Holy Ghost

Amen and Amen
Copyright © 2008

Authority of Prayer

A prayer of Mark Berryhill

I sought you because I love you; says the Almighty, seek My face.

When you were abased because of your trespasses against Me, did I not reach down from Heaven and forgive you and set you on high, seek My face.

As the beauty of a young tender child praying to Me, so is the beauty of My love for all of My children, both young and old, therefore seek My face.

As the wind passes through the needles of the great pine trees and causes music of pleasantness to the ears, so are your prayers pleasing to Me, seek My face.

In the name of the
Father, the Son and
the Holy Ghost

Amen and Amen
Copyright © 2008

A Walk with Jesus

A song of Mark Berryhill

Jehovah spread forth the Heavens by the power of His right hand, and He will soon do it again.

Jehovah said let light be, and she came into existence; He will soon do it again.

Jehovah is sovereign and supreme; He is not in need of the council of men.

Jehovah formed you in the womb of your mother, and clothed you in a suit of flesh; nothing is too difficult for Him.

Jehovah is brilliant beyond what the human mind can consider; trust Him with all of your heart, soul, and mind and strength.

In the name of the
Father, the Son and
the Holy Ghost

Amen and Amen
Copyright © 2008

Day of Salvation

A song of Mark Berryhill

Holy Father, thank You for the beauty of today.

Holy Father, thank You for each breath of life that you will provide Your people today.

Holy Father, thank You for the warmth presented to us by the sun today.

Holy Father, thank You for loving Your people with all of Your heart, soul, mind and strength today.

Holy Father, most of all, thank You for the victory of the cross of Your Son Jesus Christ, and may this writing touch the heart of someone, even this very day.

In the name of the
Father, the Son and
the Holy Ghost

Amen and Amen
Copyright © 2008

In His Presence

A song of Mark Berryhill

His precious daughter gently whispers, Abba, Abba and Jehovah quickly responds, here I AM!

His faithful son calls out, Abba, Abba and Jehovah quickly responds, here I AM!

The aged woman gently whispers, Abba, Abba and Jehovah quickly responds, here I AM!

The faithful son is now a man that has seen many years, and he still calls unto his Abba, and Jehovah still quickly responds, here I AM!

In the name of the
Father, the Son and
the Holy Ghost

Amen and Amen
Copyright © 2008

A Time of Urgency

A prayer of Mark Berryhill

When you have lost all that you own because you mortgaged your soul to the enemy, explain to Me why My lambs were not fed the Gospel of My Son Jesus Christ, states the Almighty!

When you plead for comfort because of the horrific pain that will soon come upon you because of your wickedness, explain to Me why My lambs were not fed the Gospel of My Son Jesus Christ, states the Almighty!

While your enemies slaughter your young and old before your eyes, explain to Me why My lambs were not fed the Gospel of My Son Jesus Christ, states the Almighty!

While I watch your children burn in the fires that burn your whoring cities to the ground, explain to Me why My lambs were not fed the Gospel of My Son Jesus Christ, states the Almighty!

In the name of the
Father, the Son and
the Holy Ghost

Amen and Amen
Copyright © 2008

Intent of His Heart

A song of Mark Berryhill

Why do you speak when you should listen precious son of the Most High?
Why do you speak when you should listen beautiful daughter of the Most High?
Have you written The Word of Your Father upon your heart today precious son?
Have you written The Word of Your Father upon your heart today beautiful daughter?
Serving Jesus Christ is the most important thing for you to do today precious son.
Serving Jesus Christ is the most important thing for you to do today beautiful daughter.

In the name of the
Father, the Son and
the Holy Ghost

Amen and Amen
Copyright © 2008

A Faithful Creator

A prayer of Mark Berryhill

The beauty of the rising sun is as a glimpse of the beauty of the paradise JEHOVAH is preparing for His faithful children.

The majesty of white capped mountains that reach into the Heavens offer yet another glimpse as to the paradise JEHOVAH is preparing for His faithful children.

Racing streams of JEHOVAH are singing songs of prosperity as they race down majestic mountains.

Mothers clothed in dresses of elegance, and beautiful daughters clothed in dresses of beauty, sing a song as one voice to the Creator of life, and yet another glimpse of the beauty of Heaven is shed forth.

In the name of the
Father, the Son and
the Holy Ghost

Amen and Amen
Copyright © 2008

From Everlasting to Everlasting

A prayer of Mark Berryhill

The stars are singing a new song to JEHOVAH, while the planets bow down before Him.

Prayers of precious little boys and darling daughters bring a smile to the face of the Great JEHOVAH.

His love and faithfulness is from everlasting to everlasting, and nothing or no one can pluck you from His hand.

He that is in you is greater than he that is in the world, and those who turn many to a life of righteousness will shine even as the stars.

In the name of the
Father, the Son and
the Holy Ghost

Amen and Amen
Copyright © 2008

A Dance with God

A song of Mark Berryhill

Love is the greatest of all gifts, and God is love.

Joy is placed into the heart of the believer by the Holy Ghost, and she walks beside comfort.

Peace will ultimately reign because Jesus Christ is the Prince of Peace.

Longsuffering is an attribute of the Great I AM, help us Lord to be more like You.

Gentleness leads swiftly, although there also is a time for harshness.

Goodness is brightly manifested in the children of faith.

Faith in Jesus Christ and in His name produces virtue and power.

Meekness is as patience, humble and slow to anger.

Temperance can be translated as self-control, especially in abstinence from intoxicants.

In the name of the
Father, the Son and
the Holy Ghost

Amen and Amen
Copyright © 2008

My Friend Jesus

A song of Mark Berryhill

If you need a friend who will never forsake you, call unto Jesus.

If you find yourself overextended financially, call unto Jesus and He will carry you.

If your world seems to be falling on top of you, call unto Jesus and He will save you.

If everything in your life is good, make it even better, seek Jesus.

In the name of the
Father, the Son and
the Holy Ghost

Amen and Amen
Copyright © 2008

Laughter of a Child

A song of Mark Berryhill

The precious child has neither a father nor a mother; will you raise the child as your own?

The precious child is weeping and neither father nor mother can be found; will you raise the child as your own?

The precious child has no one and is in need; will you raise the child as your own?

The precious child is laughing and comforted in the presence of a new father and a new mother; the child is found.

In the name of the
Father, the Son and
the Holy Ghost

Amen and Amen
Copyright © 2008

Life Eternal

A prayer of Mark Berryhill

Jehovah sent His Son to die for your sins; His name is Jesus Christ.
Jehovah is love, and in the blood of His Son Jesus Christ eternal life is found.
Is your great grandfather still walking on the earth?
Is your great grandmother still walking on the earth?
Jehovah sent His Son to die for your sins; His name is Jesus Christ.
Jehovah is love, and in the blood of His Son Jesus Christ eternal life is found.

In the name of the
Father, the Son and
the Holy Ghost

Amen and Amen
Copyright © 2008

Heart of JEHOVAH

A song of Mark Berryhill

Is your heart right with the heart of the great JEHOVAH?

Is your heart filled with love for other people as is the heart of JEHOVAH?

Is your heart walking in the joy and comfort offered by the right hand of the great JEHOVAH?

Is your heart in perfect union and communion with the heart of JEHOVAH?

In the name of the
Father, the Son and
the Holy Ghost

Amen and Amen
Copyright © 2008

His Sheep know His Voice

A song of Mark Berryhill

The most valuable commodity known to the human race is time.
She can be used properly as God has directed in His Word, or she can be wasted as she is currently being wasted by our nation.
For many years the Spirit of God has pleaded for His lambs to be fed His Word daily in our public schools.
Please obey the lead of the Holy Spirit by helping Him transform our public schools into the greatest daily training facilities of His Word there has ever been.

In the name of the
Father, the Son and
the Holy Ghost

Amen and Amen
Copyright © 2008

An Eternal Love

A song of Mark Berryhill

Immanuel will sing over you this very night because of His immense love for you.

Immanuel will dance over you this very night because of His immense love for you.

Immanuel forms these precious and innocent children in the wombs of their mothers because of His immense love for the children.

Immanuel, raise up a generation of people that want to seek Your face every moment of every day!

Immanuel, can Your immense love for these precious and innocent children be either weighed or measured; He softly responds, My precious child it is immeasurable.

In the name of the
Father, the Son and
the Holy Ghost

Amen and Amen
Copyright © 2008

Printed in the United States
By Bookmasters